THROUGH THE EYES

of a

GOOD GUY

A FRANK DISCUSSION ABOUT "GOOD GUY" HUSBANDS, RELATIONSHIPS AND THE AMAZING POWER OF A WIFE'S TOUCH

DOUG KENDALL

Heartflame Publishing
500 S 4th St, PO Box 2705
Hartsville, SC 29551
USA

(paperback) ISBN 979-8-9895301-0-6
(ebook) ISBN 979-8-9895301-1-3

First Edition
2024

Dedicated to my parents, grandparents, and the church family of my youth for leading me in the way I should go. When I grew older, I did not depart from it.

Thanks to Debbie Erwin and Sherry Mobley.

Very special thanks to Lesli F. Hall.

Thanks—with hot fudge, whipped cream and a cherry—to my mother, Diann Murphy, and my father, Roy Douglas Kendall. I love you.

FOREWORD (RANDOM THOUGHTS)

Because there are forces at work in politics, television, radio, music, magazines, books, movies, and more that are trying their best to glamourize and normalize infidelity, end the nuclear family, destroy the Church, and divide us all on every level possible—so that we are all spread thin, and much easier to conquer and subjugate—I feel that it is more important than ever to keep marriages and families healthy and strong, so that they remain intact during tough times.

The stories and perspectives contained within are very frank, comical, raw, funny, sad, random, painful, sarcastic, politically incorrect, written in a conversational style, and delivered with good intentions—and a lot of tough love.

Read this book, aloud, with your spouse, and discuss the situations presented in each chapter. Calm, open, honest, respectful, nonconfrontational communication is vitally important. Don't accuse, point fingers, or cop a self-righteous attitude with your spouse, because no one is perfect; we all have areas of opportunity for improvement. If you read something that gives you pause, and you feel the need to make positive changes, take the initiative to improve.

Marriage is a four-letter word: w-o-r-k. Both you and your spouse have to devote a lot of quality time and effort to your relationship, or it could eventually fail. And while this book was written mainly for women, I discuss plenty of things that men should work on, too.

When I speak of past sexual encounters, I am not attempting to glorify them, or myself (I do not condone premarital sex); I am simply stating what was going on in my life at the time, how I viewed it, and how it affected me. In order for you to better understand the gravity of the situation, and get a better idea of what happened, I go into some detail.

Even though I was raised in church, and come from a line of pastors and ministers, there was a long period of time when I lived my life outside of all that, doing whatever I wanted to do. Since I got back into church a few years ago, and started getting into ministry work, I deeply regret my past, and feel that some of the negative things that have happened in my life are directly due to my past immoral behavior. I believe in God, and that He always gives people a choice of whether or not to follow His teachings and Commandments, but I also believe there's a price to be paid for choosing not to do so.

If everything you read and value has to be crafted in some homogenized, cookie-cutter, Flavor of the Month mold that doesn't push your beliefs and boundaries, this isn't the book for you. On the other hand, if you want some straightforward, tough-love opinions from the mind of a Good Guy, read on.

Since this is a book about Good Guys, life and relationships, I will be devoting a good bit of print space to something that most guys feel is very important in marriage: sexual intimacy. I will attempt to explain why I feel it can be so important to men, how a man's emotional processes can often be very different from that of a woman's, and how women can use their feminine power to connect on a deeper level with their Good Guys. A surprisingly large percentage of women enjoy frequent lovemaking, too, so this isn't just for the guys.

I don't like the term "sex" to describe marital sexual intercourse. To me, "sex" is what you get from casual sex (also commonly referred to as a "one-night stand")—a simple, no-strings-attached, brief, emotionally-disconnected, ultimately unfulfilling, physical release. "Lovemaking," on the other hand, is a term I personally prefer to use to describe an incredible, emotional and physical connection between husband and wife, during times of sexual intimacy.

There are many differences between men and women—emotional, physical, mental and social. This book will explore some of those differences, in an effort to bring greater understanding. Hopefully, some of the ideas and opinions in this book will inspire you to overcome the hurdles and challenges that sometimes stand in the way of enjoying a happy, fulfilling marriage.

If one of you has issues in the bedroom, both of you have issues in the bedroom—no matter how unimportant or silly those issues may seem to you—and sexual intimacy in your marriage isn't going to be as good as it could be, until those issues are expressed, acknowledged and thoughtfully addressed.

Attraction can come from many things: body chemistry, visual appeal, emotional appeal, someone's voice, perceived qualities and abilities, the scent of a person, and more. Love, on the other hand, is a choice. You don't have a lot of control over attraction, but you can always choose to love someone, and be a part of someone's life, regardless of how difficult things may be between you. It is this powerful ability, to choose love—and also choose to let yourself be loved—that can save your relationship, and possibly your life.

As humans, we share many of the same desires and needs, but each person, and marriage, is unique. While this book may help many husbands and wives understand some of what makes their spouse tick, it will not fit every person, relationship or situation. Only you can determine if the personal opinions and perspectives contained within this book will be helpful and inspiring. But even if they do give you some ideas for positive change, just reading about them won't be enough; you actually have to continually work to improve, try new things, and cultivate changes within yourself, your spouse and your marriage.

If your marriage is failing, you may want to rethink doing the same things you've always done, day after day, month after month, year after year, expecting a different result! Instead of constantly fighting against your spouse, try fighting for your spouse and your marriage. This is a new day, so make the decision to humble yourself, put your ego aside, pray for God's wisdom and strength, then move in a positive, new direction for the sake of your relationship. Don't wait until it's too late, and pay the price for inaction!

At the end of this book, I include two short information profile pages for you and your spouse. After you've finished reading the book (together), fill in the blank areas, so that you will both have good ideas for gifts, date nights, vacations, special occasions, meals, surprises, and more. There's also space for your birthdays and wedding anniversary. So, if you ever need a reminder, just flip to the back of the book.

When reading this book, imagine you and I are having our regular Saturday lunch with some of our good friends, and our conversation turns to life, love, relationships and marriage. The words written on these pages are my part in those conversations, nothing more. I am not a doctor, counselor, psychologist, psychiatrist, sociologist, clinician, life coach, self-help guru, attorney or anything of the sort, and I am not giving medical advice, mental health advice, financial advice, treatment advice, scientific research, diagnosis, legal advice or counseling of any kind. I am simply sharing some of my personal views and perspectives on life and relationships. My personal views are not intended to replace advice, therapy, diagnosis, assessment, or treatment recommendations from a qualified, licensed professional; therefore, you should regard everything in this book as a personal opinion statement, and you should consult with a licensed professional before attempting anything written in this book. Please read my Disclaimer on the copyright page.

I am far from perfect, so this book is just as much for me as anyone else. As I was writing it, I discovered a number of things that I personally needed to improve, also. I made a lot of positive changes, and now I'm a much better man than I was, because of it. I hope you will be inspired to do the same.

Action without information is dangerous, and information without action is worthless. Here is some information. The action is up to you—and **at your own risk.**

CONTENTS

CHAPTER 1

A KNIGHT IN SHINING ARMOR

L adies, for purposes of this book the Good Guy is very traditional. He would never cheat, or become abusive. He's great with the kids. He always shows up for work. He's sweet, and at least *tries* to be romantic—even if he's a bit awkward, clumsy or unintentionally amusing when trying to do so, sometimes.

He remembers your birthday and wedding anniversary. He takes out the trash, helps with the dishes, is charitable, and might be a homebody.

He may not be a handyman, but he is intelligent, skilled and knowledgeable in other areas. He is protective of you and the children. You may even refer to him as being a "big teddy bear"—or maybe he's not a big guy, physically, but he has a big heart.

He's a man of Faith, or at least he has a good, moral personal code, and a strong sense of honor; he's a gentleman.

This book will assume that you value those traits, and that you have chosen a man who possesses at least a few of them. Never forget those good qualities, because they can be a lifeline for your relationship if things get tough.

Even with all of your guy's good qualities, your marriage is strained, or you've become distant, and you don't look at your husband quite the same way you used to. He may not look at *you* the same way, either, and sometimes you just don't understand each other, or feel loved. You may not even know exactly how or why things got to this point, but you know things just aren't the same, anymore.

You're not alone.

◦§◦

Back in my grandparents' day, they didn't date; they "courted." Basically, the young gentleman would go to the young lady's home, where everything was under careful watch of her family.

The couple would sit apart from each other, and they would simply talk and get to know one another. There was no making out, or anything of the sort; even holding hands was often considered inappropriate.

The point of that was, first and foremost, to keep things pure and innocent, but another big point was to actually get to know the other person, before anything else moved forward. I know that "courting" is a very outdated concept—and I certainly wouldn't want *my* dates to be supervised, either—but I think there was a lot to be said for actually getting to know someone, before making any relationship decisions.

These days, it's all too common to go out for a night on the town and find someone to "hook up" (have casual sex) with. There's no love involved. It's just a brief encounter, and a physical release—and, ultimately, unsatisfying to the soul, at the end of the day.

Maybe it's just the thrill of the chase—or *being* chased—or simply a case of hormones running wild.

Sometimes people hook up and have great sex, and then they get into some type of relationship, *after* the fact, thinking that the sex was good so there has to be something there. Unfortunately, just because they have good physical chemistry with someone, it doesn't mean they're going to have a great *emotional* connection and get along.

Look at the "love/hate/love" relationships out there, where people are constantly splitting up and then getting back together, and you can get a good idea of what that's like. The sex is good, but they can't stand to be around each other for too long. They keep coming back, now and then, for sex, thinking things might be different *this* time, but nothing ever changes and they remain frustrated with each other—and apart.

This type of situation can also become a big thorn in both of their sides; never giving either of them a satisfying relationship, while also keeping them from moving on and finding *real* love with someone else.

It's an issue of chemistry vs. compatibility: Chemistry will cause the sparks to fly, and your heart to flutter, when you kiss and touch, but *compatibility* will play a big part in determining whether or not your relationship can last, and be more than just physical.

Personally, I have experienced a lot of hurt and scarring, over the years. It's a miracle that my Good Guy personality is still intact, because I could have easily gone the other way.

Actually, I did go the other way, for a little while.

Sadly, there were a couple of times in my younger days where I treated women like toilet paper; I would use them and then toss them away. Don't get me wrong; I was never abusive or hurtful, and I was always a gentleman (some things never change), but I didn't want any attachments. Some of the women wanted a relationship, but all I wanted from the encounters was the conquest and physical pleasure.

I had made up my mind to use women for my personal enjoyment and entertainment, because my heart had been broken into a million *very sharp* pieces and I didn't care about love, anymore. It was "the straw that broke the camel's back," as the saying goes. I was deeply hurt, angry and depressed.

"Love? What a joke!" I remember thinking. "I'll just get what I want and move on. I don't need love."

Boy, was I wrong!

After about two years of being a single Bad Boy, for a second time, I woke one morning with images of the previous weekend's activities floating through my mind, as I walked to the bathroom mirror.

Looking at myself, feeling drained and empty inside, I heard a voice in my head say, "That's not you. That's not who you are. You're better than that. Sleeping around doesn't make you a 'real' man. These women you're using have never done anything to hurt you; your anger is misplaced. No matter what others did to you, you always have to be true to yourself and remain in control. You're a Good Guy. Now *act* like it!"

I walked away from the mirror, and my mindset changed almost immediately—and forevermore. I ripped off the mask of hurt and anger that I had been hiding behind. I decided to—very cautiously—make myself available, again. I wasn't going to look for it, but if real love came my way, I would at least make an effort.

Not long after, I did meet someone and we were together for quite some time. Once my brain adjusted to the reality of the situation, I discovered just how wonderful a touch could be, with a woman that I loved—a woman who loved and *desired* me, the same way I desired her.

I discovered, early on, that I felt loved and emotionally-connected to a woman through physical touch (hugging, holding hands, kissing, cuddling, massaging, caressing, sex, etc.), but I came to realize that it was just a physical fix if love wasn't fueling it.

To me, sexual intimacy without love is like eating a steak that's been overcooked and charred. Yes, it's still a steak, but it hasn't been properly prepared and isn't very tasty. On the other hand, uninhibited *lovemaking* in an emotionally-strong, tightly-bonded, trusting marriage is like a perfectly cooked and seasoned ribeye—so delicious and satisfying, down to your very *soul!*

The physical part, alone, doesn't fill the emotional void, though, and the emotional part of it doesn't fill the physical void. If you want an amazing, satisfying connection with your spouse, try making *both* of them a priority.

The things that I have learned since those days—and since I have renewed my relationship with God—have given me much greater insight into how Good Guys, like me, process love, touch, dating, relationships, emotion, communication and more. Ladies, it is my hope that something in this book will help you better understand *your* Good Guy, so you can make a positive difference in your marriage.

Your Good Guy really wants you to understand more about what makes him who he is, and this is my attempt to put my personal views and opinions about Good Guys and relationships into book form.

If all you're looking for is quick and meaningless hook-ups, or if TV shows, pop songs, modern relationship websites, social influencers and trendy magazines have convinced you that extra-marital sex might "spice up your marriage," you will not find any kind of support for that in this book. I'm not built that way, and I do not condone adulterous—and potentially *marriage-ending*—behavior.

CHAPTER 2

MY STORY & BIGGEST REGRET

When I was young, I was very involved in my church. My paternal grandfather was the pastor and founder, and I had been elected president of the youth group. My mother was the pianist, my father was the Minister of Music, and my paternal grandmother was the organist.

I greatly enjoyed church youth activities, and even ran for the statewide office of youth president, in our affiliated churches. I hoped, eventually, to be a youth counselor, and help young people with life, relationships and salvation— but I made a last-minute decision to study computers, instead, unfortunately.

I absolutely *loved* (and still do) science fiction, medieval fantasy novels, comic books, role-playing games, and Heavy Metal music. On top of that, I was a scrawny, sickly, nerdy kid, so I was a very easy target for bullies, and I got picked on—sometimes, brutally—by other kids (I have physical scars).

Now, those classic sci-fi shows, heavy bands and fantasy entertainment franchises that I grew up with, and got bullied for loving, are some of the most successful of all time—and I say that with all of the smugness I can muster.

I had a *lot* of serious medical issues, and I was also a very sheltered choir boy of a kid, so I was ill-prepared for the hostile environment of public (government-run) school.

I tried to play kickball in elementary school, but would usually be the last guy picked for a team, during school recess. I also tried playing city-league baseball, but I wasn't good. I was still too frail, at that time, to be a serious contributor on any sports team.

I got my first kiss while playing my last season of baseball, and the girl who kissed me became my first girlfriend. It was just puppy love, but it was nice to know that a girl liked me, even though I wasn't as tough or strong as most of the other boys my age.

I was on all kinds of medication, and getting by, but one day I had a breakdown and started sobbing. I told my mother that I didn't care if I died; I was going to stop taking all of the medicines and weekly shots. I wanted to be like other kids, and play hard, run fast, and have fun. I was going to do it, or die trying!

She could see the anguish on my face, and knew that I was serious. She was (and still is) a very protective, loving and caring mother, so I was surprised when she let me have my way. The only stipulation was that I had to keep my "emergency" medicine.

It wasn't until I stopped taking the drugs and shots, and became more active, that I got better. I got physically stronger, and mentally tougher—and I haven't been on any prescription medications for over 30 years.

Around the age of twelve, I went back to playing miniature golf—a fun sport that my father introduced me to, when I was around four years old—and I was pretty good at it. Before I turned the age of 14, I had won four tournament trophies.

Taekwondo, a Korean martial art, became a thing for me, in an attempt to defend myself against bullies, and I did well. I was fascinated by not only the physical discipline, but the *mental* discipline that was so important, as well. I discovered that the mind could be used to help control pain and maintain focus, and that willpower was a huge asset in overcoming problems, insecurities and difficult situations.

I lettered in Band, midway through high school. I only weighed 115 pounds, and I was so skinny that the chest area of my jacket wasn't big enough to fit the letter patch that I was given. I had to get it sewn over the left-side pocket, where it had a little bit of room to wrap around my side, under my arm.

My first *real* date, in high school—where I actually drove to the girl's house and picked her up—was extremely embarrassing for me, because I didn't know anything about etiquette. I was always a gentleman, but I hadn't been taught the finer points of dating—like getting out of the car and going to the door, meeting the girl's parents, opening her car door, etc. I actually waited for her to come out and get in the car, and I didn't walk her to the door, to see her safely inside, the way a proper gentleman would. I didn't know what I was doing, and it was all very awkward for me. Thankfully, the woman, a classmate, and I are still good friends, and she has always been very understanding and forgiving.

In the halls of government, there was a political push to censor rock and rap music—along with possibly reassessing the contracts of artists who didn't obey rules that were being proposed for lyrics and album covers.

I was a singer, and now a drummer, who dreamed of touring the world in a Heavy Metal band, so government interference in music *had to be stopped!*

In the end, major record labels instituted the use of "parental advisory" labels for albums that contained explicit content—which did nothing, except make the rock and rap kids want to buy the "explicit" stuff even more! In fact, those of us who always wore black t-shirts of our favorite heavy bands began wearing shirts with the advisory label printed on them, as a badge of honor and a big slap in the face to would-be censors. (I still have my heavily-worn shirt packed away, as a reminder of those times.)

I had always been rebellious and independent, but the fight over regulating music took things to a new level and played a *big* role in my becoming opposed to government power—and I've only become more steadfast in my beliefs, since.

Even when I was still figuring out my personal philosophy, and didn't know that a name existed for it ("voluntaryism"), I knew that I went way beyond most others who claimed to be "pro-freedom."

Around that time, my parents threw away all of my hard rock and Heavy Metal albums, and role-playing game books, due to the "satanic panic" message that was making its way through churches at that time. Needless to say, I was *furious!*

Eventually, I replaced all of it—and added *much* more—but I kept it hidden and protected. I became a very private person, and I'm still quite protective of things that bring me joy and happiness.

In addition to everything else that was stressing me out, I had a few relationships that ended badly. I was very settled, at an early age, and knew that I could be a great guy for the right girl, but all of my hopes and dreams were shattered, due to some very hurtful breakups.

Eventually, I ended up in a place where it felt like my world was collapsing in on me, and I was being overwhelmed by emotions that I had not previously experienced. I was being robbed of everything that I loved and wanted, it felt like it was me against the world, and I wasn't sure that I could handle what I was feeling.

I didn't know how to stop the pain and anger, so I withdrew from those closest to me and tried to sort it all out, but I didn't do a very good job.

One particular afternoon, while I was at one of my lowest points, a friend called and heard the rage, hatred and hurt in my voice. He knew that I had been dealing with a lot, but he was surprised by my emotional state.

I ended the call, and about seven minutes later he came barreling through the front yard and slid his car right up to the front door of my house. He must have had his car flying in the wind, because he lived on the other side of town.

My friend didn't even bother knocking; he just rushed in and ran over to where I was seated on the couch. He took me by the arm and said, "You're coming with me."

I let him lead me to his car, and I just froze when I got next to it. He tried to get me to go around to the passenger's side, but I wouldn't move, so he opened the driver's side backdoor, where I stood, and pushed me toward the seat.

"Come on, get in," he pleaded. After a brief moment, I relented and sat in the back.

That's when it all hit me—that my world was completely *wrecked*—and I just fell over, on my side, in the backseat. I stayed liked that for a long time, while my friend drove me back and forth through town, hoping I would settle down.

I guess it worked, because it gave me time to process everything, and accept it. After that, I was just completely stunned, heartbroken, directionless and lonely.

I hated myself for looking so weak in front of my friend, because guys weren't supposed to get emotional—at least, that was the message most guys received, back then, when I was growing up.

I let my straight, brown hair grow halfway down my back, learned just enough guitar to be able to write some heavy songs, started playing drums in rock bands, and I bought a motorcycle. My life revolved around music, concerts and trips to the coast.

A few years later, I tried another relationship. It was never really good, and it ended very badly. I grew up very quickly, and learned even more about the ways of the world.

I became very outspoken, bolder, tougher, angrier and cold. I kept most of my life hidden away, so that no one could interfere, ever again. I also decided that I would refrain from self-censoring, and live my life any way that I wanted.

If I felt that someone was trying to bully, pick on, take advantage of, look down on, or target me, I pushed back, *harder*. I was never going to let anyone do that to me, again.

It got to the point where my concerned mother said to me, "You don't smile, anymore. It's like you've got a big chip on your shoulder, waiting for someone to knock it off." I was completely and unapologetically truthful with her when I replied, "I do."

After all that I had been through in life—health problems, being bullied, heartbreaks, fake friends, people around me trying to change and control me, and more—I didn't really care any longer. I became one of the Bad Boys, running wild, doing exactly what I wanted to do, regardless of any moral compass. I decided to stop dwelling on negative emotions, loosen up, turn things around and play the field.

Nearly every weekend, I was meeting a new girl—or girls—and having some type of physical encounter. The girls wanted attention and excitement, and I wanted a physical connection, so things usually worked out.

My favorite spots were a beach, a lake, and a hotel with a large pool. Any time I got near enough to a large body of water to hear the waves roll in, I felt relaxed and peaceful—and bringing a girl along was just icing on the cake.

There were many times when I booked an ocean-view room for myself and a girl, or I took a girl to a local lake for some skinny-dipping. A few times, though, I simply parked by the water for a make-out session.

I knew all along that what I was doing was morally unacceptable, according to my Christian values, but I never let myself think much about it. I paid a heavy price for those things, and I broke a couple of hearts along the way, too, unfortunately. I was too bitter to really care, though.

A couple of years before all of that, I had seen a beautiful girl working in a local record store, when a friend of mine and I went to look for some new music. She was absolutely *gorgeous*, with long, reddish-brown hair, beautiful blue eyes, a bright smile, and a bubbly personality. My brain took a snapshot of her, the first time I saw her, and that image has remained pinned to the back of my mind since that day.

I went back to the music store, several times, but I never saw her there again, unfortunately.

Later on, I became friends with a fellow comic book nerd, and I was stunned when I found out that the pretty girl from the music store was his girlfriend!

Even though I was attracted to her, I never said a word about it, or did anything to disrespect my friend and his relationship with her. In fact, I went out of my way to keep things pure and innocent.

She and Comic Book Buddy eventually broke up, but she and I remained close, and we became best friends. She was a ray of sunshine—a sunbeam—shining brightly in my dark world, and my life was so much better with her in it.

During the time I was playing the Bad Boy, she would always call me on Monday morning, and wake me, to ask about what kind of trouble I had gotten into over the weekend. I would tell her all about my dirty deeds, and she would attempt to be a positive influence. I could tell she was shaking her head at me, and facepalming, even over the phone.

Though I have always been a "night owl," staying up late and sleeping in, I always loved it when Sunbeam called. She was the only person who could get away with calling me so early, and still put a smile on my face. Purposefully and regularly calling me, while I was still in bed, seemed very intimate and special—and quite *bold*, on her part. I didn't experience that with anyone else.

I really enjoyed hanging out, talking on the phone and taking little road trips with her. I even loved hearing her pretty voice, so just talking to her was a pleasure. She was truly my brightest light.

Even though I had walled-off my emotions, she had gotten through my defenses, and I was having difficulty with the feelings that I had developed for her.

I played the role of big brother, and I always had her safety, happiness and well-being in mind. She was strong-willed, intelligent, independent, and could take care of herself pretty well, when necessary, but I was always happy to help if she wanted or needed it.

Looking back on it, I think I used the big brother vibe as an emotional defense mechanism, to keep everything in check and set the tone for the type of relationship that couldn't hurt me as bad if things went sour. I was secretly *very* attracted to her, but I didn't do anything about it, because I was scared that something would get screwed up and I would be left with *nothing*.

In the end, I decided that I would rather have her as my best friend than to take a chance on a relationship ending badly and not having her in my life, at all—and, for that, I want to kick myself. Very hard. Repeatedly.

I remember both of us being at a local club, one weekend night. As I was talking with some friends, she quickly walked over to me, because a guy kept trying to hit on her. She put her arm around me, and nicely told the other guy that she was with *me*. It was unexpected, but I liked it. A lot.

The guy apologized and shook my hand. He said he wasn't aware that we were together, and he wasn't trying to cause any trouble. I played along, was very gracious, and told the guy that everything was cool. After he walked away, she thanked me for "saving" her.

It felt really good for her to trust in me that way, to let me come to her aid, knowing without a doubt that I would be there for her any time she needed me. It also left a lasting impression on me, as you can tell.

She may have been trying to send a message to *me*, as well, with that gesture, but men aren't mind readers— something I will address, in more detail, later in this book.

She and I were very close, and could talk about *anything*, but I was just too paralyzed by past hurt and fear to take a chance on what was right in front of me—and I have no doubt that we would have made a terrific, life-long couple, if I hadn't been so scared and guarded.

I remember an evening trip we took to the beach, in her car. It was a cool, Autumn night, and we talked all the way there (almost a two-hour drive).

When we got to our destination, we walked, holding hands, to an ocean pier. We leaned against the railing, while watching the waves crashing in, and continued talking for a while, enjoying each other's company.

At one point, as we were enjoying the view and sounds of the waves, there was a brief moment of silence. We turned to each other at the same instant and made eye contact—one of those moments you see in romantic movies where time stands still and everything just clicks into place. I never would have believed that the movie magic stuff happens in real life, if I hadn't experienced it for myself.

In that split second, my head began having a very heated argument with my heart.

My heart was saying, "Doug, you had better kiss that lovely girl, *right now*, if you know what's good for you! This is what you've wanted! You two are *great* together! Don't you see it? What are you waiting for?!"

My head, on the other hand, was saying, "Don't do it! You know how women are, and how most relationships end these days; a beautiful friendship will eventually be ruined, and she will be completely lost to you, *forever!* Women lie and cheat! Just keep playing the field and having fun! Turn away, *now!*"

In that split second—which felt like an eternity in my mind—my head won the fight, and I turned back toward the ocean. Not long after that, she mentioned that we should probably head back, so we walked to her car and made our way home.

I remember us parking next to my car, which I had left in a shopping center parking lot. As we were sitting there, still talking, she was stretching, tired and aching from a long ride in the driver's seat. She leaned forward against the steering wheel, and I reached over to give her an innocent shoulder and back massage.

The instant I touched her shoulders, something *clicked*, as if a power switch had been flipped on inside me. With any of my other female friends, it would have just been another innocent backrub, to help a buddy relax and loosen up. This was completely different, though, because it was *her.*

I was in heaven, with her accepting and enjoying my touch, trusting me, and allowing me to take her body into my hands and make her feel better. The chemistry was *definitely* there, and I felt a very strong connection to her.

The only way I can describe it is to say that touching her in that way was absolutely *electrifying* and energizing. I was no longer tired; my senses were heightened, and she became my sole focus. The rest of the world could have ended and disappeared, and I wouldn't have noticed.

Feeling her softness in my hands, being fully aware of the beautiful lines and curves of her body—and seeing her relaxing, and enjoying what I was doing to her—made me feel like I was the master of the universe. I hadn't felt so strongly about a woman in a long time.

I wanted to run my fingers through her hair, scoop her over into my arms and kiss her slowly and deeply, right then and there. I wanted her to be the sole beneficiary of every good thing I had to offer in this life, and I wanted her to be mine, forever.

Then fear and doubt hit me, again. I regretfully backed off, knowing I was missing another incredible opportunity.

After we had wished each other a good night, and as I was making my exit from her car, I heard my heart *screaming* at me, in a last-ditch effort to convince me to get back in the car, kiss her passionately and make her mine. Once again, though, my head triumphed.

Many years later, I found her and we renewed our friendship. She was married, with kids, and I was genuinely happy for her and the family life that she had made. (I still only want the best for her, always.)

Reconnecting was eventually bound to happen, because, according to her, we've always had a "silver string" tying us together. I believe it, because certain things about us can only be explained by our spiritual connection.

We talked about her family, her life's journey, and reminisced about days gone by. I eventually confided that I had wanted to date her, but I messed it all up; I was scared, and didn't want to take a chance of ruining a great friendship, or getting hurt again.

In a nerdy way that did not disrespect her marriage, or give any indication that she would ever do anything to jeopardize it (I appreciated that loyalty to her husband), she joked about an alternate universe, where our alternate selves were married and had the average 2.5 kids, and all that silly stuff.

She also mentioned the big brother vibe, which gave her the impression that I hadn't viewed her in a romantic way. Hearing *that*, my heart sank, and I wanted to kick myself, again!

During one of our conversations, I asked her what happened to cause us to lose touch. She was surprised that I didn't remember.

She said that she called, one morning, as usual, and a woman who was in bed with me answered the call.

After that, my Sunbeam never called again to wake me, and we eventually moved on with our lives and drifted apart.

If I correctly interpreted all of the signs and signals from her, I missed out on an amazing, beautiful, intelligent, loving, supportive, fiery woman, because of fear, anger, hurt, self-centeredness and doubt.

Many other Good Guys out there have been badly hurt, too. They still carry around nasty scars, and hearts that weren't put back together very well, after they were broken.

Men who have suffered heartbreak, humiliation and other types of emotional—and sometimes physical—trauma are probably going to carry some of that baggage with them into future relationships. These men have to learn to trust again.

If you are involved with such a man, show him that you truly love him, and that he can trust you without any doubt. One little "white lie," or cover-up—no matter how small you may think it to be—could bring all your progress crashing down, or break you up.

A lot of men don't talk much about their feelings, and they hold things inside. They don't want to admit that they were hurt, tricked, abused, etc., so help them see that they can love and trust again, and be happy.

I'm not saying to wait around forever, because there comes a point where a man has to make a decision to help himself and grow (and women have to do the same thing, too!), but understand that it may take a little time and encouragement.

In my story, above, if my Sunbeam had come to me and lovingly put it all on the table, telling me that she wanted to be my girl and stand with me through thick and thin, to take a chance on us, and work tirelessly to keep us together—or if *she* had kissed *me*, that night in her car—I think the trajectory of my life would have been forever changed.

Looking back on it all, I realize now that she could have taken my heart, so very easily. I don't think either of us realized, then, just how much potential *power* she had in my world. All I needed was for her to say what she felt, and remove all doubt, and I would have been her fearless Knight in Shining Armor, forever willing to put my life on the line for her safety and happiness.

Apparently, she was just as scared, so neither of us acted on anything, unfortunately.

I'm so very happy that our persistent connection—and individual "orbits," as she calls them—brought us back around to each other, when we were both in dark places and needed each other's support the most. We're still best friends, but our paths in life—at least, in *this* universe—went in different directions.

Making a real love connection often requires someone to be courageous and take a risk, and either of us could have done so, in my story. Instead, we let fear and doubt destroy any chance we may have had.

So don't wait around! Let your scarred Good Guy know how much he is loved and valued by you—and don't just say it, also *show* it.

Time, understanding, trust and nurturing can often heal old wounds.

CHAPTER 3

READ THIS <u>VERY</u> CAREFULLY

Never say "Happy wife, happy life" again! Change it to "Happy spouse, happy house!"

Personally, I feel that it's imperative to make that wording change—and, more importantly, the mindset and behavioral changes that must go along with it—because husband and wife should *both* work to make each other happy and satisfied. Marriage isn't solely about one person's needs, wants, satisfaction and happiness; there's another person in the relationship who has needs, feelings, desires, weaknesses, strengths and more, too.

Husband and wife are *equally* important, and should treat each other that way.

CHAPTER 4

THEY SAY THAT NICE GUYS FINISH LAST

A fter being hurt by a Bad Boy, women sometimes ask, "Where have all the good guys gone?" When they ask that question, my head feels like it's going to explode!

Where have all the good guys gone? *Seriously?!* They've quietly gone into their secret underground bunkers, to guard themselves from ever feeling the pain of heartbreak again!

There are many sad stories of women breaking up with, or cheating on, a Good Guy to be with a Bad Boy. When the Bad Boy crushes the woman's heart, hopes and dreams—or abuses her—she often cries for the Good Guy to come back, but the Good Guy's heart and trust have been destroyed, so he's often long gone and out of reach.

Guys, as opposed to the ways the Bad Boys use women for their selfish purposes, use your skills, talents and abilities for *good* things. Be the confidante, protector, gentleman, best friend and committed partner that your lady needs you to be.

Traditional wives don't seem to respect weak-willed, pushover husbands that they can walk all over—but they don't want cocky jerks, either. They want principled, masculine men who possess quiet confidence, inner strength, courage and conviction—men who will lead their families in the right direction and stand firm in the face of danger.

Bottom line: Your wife wants to feel safe and secure.

If something in the home breaks down, take the initiative to have it repaired or replaced.

Spend quality time with your children. Love them, laugh with them, compliment them, support them, be a positive role model for them, be their hero, show them how to protect themselves, read the Bible and pray with them, help them cultivate healthy self-esteem, and contribute to their positive growth—and watch as your wife's heart warms for you. Children who have a positive self-image, and grow up with strong, positive role models, tend to be better at avoiding those who would try to use, abuse or manipulate them.

Schedule a "family night," each week, to strengthen the bonds between all of you. Share what's going on in your lives, while playing games or doing other fun things together.

Regularly pray with your wife, and work together with her on household budgeting, financial goals, personal goals, vacation details and long-range plans—and keep each other accountable. Your wife wants to feel *financially* secure, too.

Be firm and consistent (but not mean, intimidating, loud, or heavy-handed) with the rules that protect your kids. *Lovingly* let them know that your rules are there to keep them from harm, or keep them away from destructive influences, and that you put those rules in place because you love them dearly and never want anything bad to happen to them.

If your resolve is tested, remain calm, cool, and collected. *Always* be a gentleman, but stand strong on the things that you feel are important for the continued good health of your marriage and family.

True masculinity isn't "toxic," and it isn't about being intimidating, bullying, or beating someone in a fistfight; it's about strength of *character*, and being a gentle giant, or lighthouse in any storm, for your family.

Masculinity can be extremely important for remaining calm, focused, getting to the root of a problem, finding a solution, and then having the strength of will to do what is necessary to protect, provide for and comfort loved ones.

Refuse to be the Good Guy who finishes in last place. Be a loving, protective, committed family man, and you could enjoy a great love life, well-adjusted kids and a supportive wife, while other guys are complaining about their unruly children and failing marriages.

CHAPTER 5

MEN ARE NOT MIND READERS

W e don't do well with hints, either.
This is one of the most common problem-causing issues between men and women, so please pay very close attention as I drop some profound wisdom upon you.

Ready? Here it is: If you want a man to understand something, you just need to come right out and *say* it. Be straight up about it, so there will be no room for misunderstandings.

Yes! I can see the clouds part, as a ray of sunshine illuminates your face, and the angels sing and harmonize with "*Ahhhhh!*" as it all makes sense to you, now.

I know; who am I kidding, right? So much for the straight-forward approach.

Example:

Her: "You remember Marjorie, from my office? Her birthday is Friday, and her sister is throwing a surprise party for her that night. I'm going, and you're invited, too—if you want to come."

Him: "Thanks, but I might get together with Jason on Friday. I haven't seen him in several weeks. I don't really know Marjorie that well, anyway."

Her: (Demeanor changes, visibly disappointed)

Him: "Hey, what's wrong? Are you mad at me?"

Her: (Walking away) "It's no big deal."

Him: (Following her) "Clearly, it *is* a big deal. I take it you didn't like my answer."

Her: (Stops, sighs and turns to him) "It's just that we don't go out as much as we used to, so I really wanted us to go to the party *together*."

Him: "Why didn't you just say so? You made it sound like it was my choice to make, but I will be happy to go with you."

Her: "No, I don't want you to, now. You already said you might have other plans, and I don't want you to change them just because I said something. Go hang out with Jason and have a good time."

Him: "No, wait a second. This is really messed up. If I go with you, you're going to be ill and act like a charity case. Night ruined—and probably the next couple of days, too. If I *don't* go, you're going to be mad that I didn't go with you. Again, night ruined—and then some. No matter what I do, I can't win!"

(They argue.)

She wanted him to choose to go with her to the party, as his *first* choice, without her having to say it. She had already worked the scenario out in her head, but there was no way he could have known about those plans, unless she had told him from the start.

He, on the other hand, thought that he was truly being given a choice. (Ha! Silly boy.)

Let's try it again, but change things up just a little.

Her: "Do you remember Marjorie, from my office? Her birthday is Friday, and her sister is throwing a surprise party for her that night. I'm going, and I would really love it if you would go with me, since we haven't had time to go out much, lately. *After* the party," she moves close to him, wraps her arms around his neck, looks him in the eyes, smiles and speaks playfully and seductively, "we could come back home and have our own *private* party."

Him: "Ooh, I like the sound of that!" he says as he smiles and wraps his arms around her waist. "Count me in!"

They kiss, and not one mention of him hanging out with Jason. (Sorry, Jason. Wife, wanting to make love, wins.)

Did you see what happened? The wife got her wish of spending a wonderful evening with her Good Guy husband, just by changing a few words. She was smart and *powerful*, because she found a way to give *both* of them the type of connection that each of them valued the most.

For her, it was socializing and connecting with friends, and spending quality time with her man. For him, it was being able to support her desire to be together and socialize, and knowing that they would be spending some quality time together, *alone*, later.

Before you get the wrong idea, lovemaking should never be thought of as a reward or treat, to manipulate your husband into doing what you want him to do. It's definitely *not* a reward or treat; it's the way he connects with you, emotionally, and he really wants that connection. (More on that, later.)

Believe it or not, your Good Guy wants to spend time with you, but what he initially thought in the first scenario was, "Party. I don't really know Marjorie, or the others in her office, that well. It will be awkward for me. She'll probably be preoccupied with her coworkers, and talk about office stuff. I won't have a good time, and I'll come home mentally exhausted."

Your husband often sees things differently, and he doesn't get all of the long-range plans you've dreamed up, unless you share them with him—and he dares not presume, lest he make a mistake and fuel your irritation, when he could have just kept his mouth shut and probably stood a better chance of coming out unscathed.

Is your husband *scared* of your irritation and anger? No. He just doesn't want to have to *deal* with it. It's exhausting, and makes him not want to be around you.

In the second scenario, because of open and honest communication, the man's perspective changed to this: "Okay, party. I don't really know Marjorie, or the others in the office, but my wife wants to make it a date night, too, so I know we'll interact, be flirty with each other, and have a good time together. I won't be able to take my mind off of her and what we're going to enjoy together, later. She's amazing, and I love the way she lets me know that she wants me. I will be *dying* to get her home, alone, but I'll try to make sure she has fun at the party, first."

You see, delivery is *everything!*

Don't hint. Don't assume. Don't wait for him to get a clue. Just be open about what you want and how you feel!

You say, "But I don't want to have to tell him everything, all the time. I want him to *get it*, and do something, without me having to spell it out for him!"

Personally, I would rather be told exactly what's going on, so we can try to make things better between us—and, hopefully, learn and grow along the way. It's certainly better than the alternative (silence, distance and resentment)!

In a perfect world, hints would be enough and everyone would be happy—but this isn't a perfect world. Again, men can't read minds.

You may have to decide which one is more important to you: being open and honest about what you want (which will probably ensure that you get it), or waiting around and hoping that he will get your hint—and most likely ending up in a fight, if he doesn't.

Good Guy husbands should, of course, also make an effort, and take mental notes of their wife's behavior patterns, speech and clues, so they are better able to decipher any hidden messages, in the future. This isn't all on the shoulders of the wives; the Good Guy husbands have work to do, too!

By the way, guys, if your wife has your full attention, looks you in the eyes and says "You're invited, too," it's a good bet that she wants you to join her.

CHAPTER 6

HE MARRIED <u>YOU</u>

Not your mother. Or your father. Or your brothers, sisters, aunts, uncles, or cousins. And he *definitely* didn't marry your friends! Same goes for *his* family and friends, too. He didn't marry your family; he married *into* your family.

Your marriage is between you and your husband, only! No one else should get into your marriage business and tell you how to manage it. You are adults. Both of you should handle your issues, on your own, *together*.

That doesn't mean that you two, as a couple, can't ask for help from friends and family, especially if those people have a proven track record of giving you great, constructive criticism and helpful advice. It simply means that you and your husband should make all of the final decisions, no matter what others may say—and *contrary* to what others say, if you are convinced that your way is the best way.

At the end of the day, no one else has to wake up and live with the consequences of the decisions that you and your husband make for yourselves. You two are the ones who have to live with them, so you should make them, together.

Unless both you *and* your husband honestly welcome and value external input from family and friends, think very carefully before allowing other people to get involved in your personal business.

CHAPTER 7

<u>ALL</u> WOMEN ARE CRAZY

This chapter is more for the guys, because men sometimes joke about women being crazy—and some of my female friends laugh and agree—so I decided to have a little bit of fun with it.

I thought about designing *Doug's Crazy Women Chart*, detailing some of the crazy types, making it look all scientific and stuff (it's not), with a formal diagram and layout. I even thought about adding some flowers, or puppy pictures, but in the end, I decided to just write it and be done with it. It's not flashy, and there are no puppy pictures, but I hope you like it, anyway.

❧

All jokes aside, I know that all women aren't stark, raving mad; there are very cool, stable, fun-loving, kind, happy women all across the world, who naturally brighten a room when they enter it. Some of them are close, very dear friends of mine, and I am very thankful that they are a part of my life.

All of us—women *and* men—have our issues, and I've written a lot about my own in this book, but I have been greatly blessed with some wonderful, supportive, female friends, and I am very thankful that they are a part of my life. Maybe I'll pick on the crazy *guys*, in the next book.

Just be careful, and watch for serious, negative behaviors, no matter who you are.

❧

<u>Tier 1 Crazy</u>: This type of wife is unwavering, and it is actually extremely rare for anything "crazy" to happen in her world. She is focused, and mentally and emotionally

stable—and that's great! Unfortunately, *nothing* happens without a plan and preparation, so *nothing* occurs outside of established routines—and certainly *nothing* spontaneous.

This type of woman is loyal, but *freakishly* methodical, and doesn't take any risks, or try new things. She is a planner and total control freak who follows strict, daily routines, and has a list and place for *everything*. Any deviation throws her world into total chaos, and she may flip out and lose her mind if circumstances force her to change her ways.

If stable, but completely inflexible, boring and routine, is what you need in your life, this Tier 1 Crazy may be a great choice for you.

Tier 2 Crazy: This is probably the "sweet spot," for me. I prefer a woman who is very emotionally stable, supportive and genuine, but also *young at heart*.

The Tier 2 Crazy is emotionally rock-solid, and you can always count on her for the important things in life, and in your marriage, but she also enjoys being a little naughty (the *good* kind) and spontaneous. She's a happy, loyal, creative, free-spirited dreamer.

This type of crazy is the adventurous "partner in crime." She's your stable wife, but also your upbeat best friend who's willing to take a little good-natured risk, here and there—and go down fighting, alongside you, if things go sideways.

She is feminine and sensual, enjoys flirting with you, and loves the quality time that you spend together. She is sexually uninhibited (little to no hang-ups or insecurities), and even likes to try new and exciting things with you, in bed.

If you like a drama-free woman who adds positive energy—and a spontaneous road trip, evening out on the town, or romantic getaway, once in a while—this might be your preferred type of wife.

This woman might also be called *The Legendary, Magical, Mystical Creature That No One Can Seem to Find.*

Tier 3 Crazy: This category includes *several* crazy types. A few of them are listed, below.

The Party Girl from Hell:

She's a wild child, lives life on the edge, is indecent, vengeful, unforgiving, unstable, sneaky and isn't going to be tied down to one person—no matter what she may promise.

She lives for the party and alcohol—usually to drown her sorrows, in her world of insecurity—to tune-out of her rotten reality. She's also a drama queen, and can be counted on to stir up trouble, or be in the middle of anything negative that gets stirred up by someone else, anywhere she goes.

Do you like getting into fights with other guys, when she purposefully starts trouble, in order to watch you fight over her? Are you okay with bailing her out of jail for being a public drunk, assaulting someone who "disrespected" her, destroying personal property, and more?

Are you fine with all of the reports you're going to get from mutual friends telling you that she was dating some other guy, this past weekend, in a neighboring town, while you were at work? If you're okay with all of that, this one's for you, champ.

The Saboteur:

Sadly, this woman doesn't have any self-worth, for one or more of a multitude of possible reasons. She will often subconsciously do things that sabotage her career, relationships, friendships, marriage, etc., and then tell herself that she is obviously unworthy of happiness and good things, because everything has come crashing down.

In relationships, she craves emotional connection and security, and things may seem to be pretty good in the beginning, but her emotions are actually walled-off, fiercely guarded and disconnected, so she will not get what she claims she wants.

She might provoke, belittle or emasculate her man, and pick his words apart, in an effort to find something (ridiculous, childish, not what he actually said or meant) to fight about. When an argument starts, because of that, she will use it as an excuse to become confrontational, justify her warped feelings and often flip out—sometimes violently.

She might recall every single thing, over many years, that the man has ever done that she didn't like—and things that her brain has erroneously convinced her that he did, in order to try to justify her feelings. She might also threaten to end the relationship—or her own life—often.

The Saboteur isn't emotionally stable enough to handle a relationship, in the first place, so she is in a constant and subconscious state of panic, looking for a way out, even though things in reality aren't like she has made them out to be in her mind. Her brain is just looking for another excuse to say that she isn't worthy. Breaking up, in her dark mind, proves it—even though the relationship was destined to fail, from the beginning, due to insecurities and self-sabotage.

The Hard Luck Woman:

The Hard Luck Woman can never catch a break. Things in her world never go the way she hopes.

The problem with this woman is that she doesn't realize that all the bad stuff in her life is happening because of her poor choices. It isn't "hard luck," at all; it's her lack of wisdom and self-discipline—and she'll desperately drag you right into the middle of it all, and cling to you for dear life, in the hope that you will drive away the dark cloud that follows her, overhead.

When you aren't able to "fix" everything and make it all better—because *she* has to be the one to change and do that—the negativity will become unbearable, and the relationship will sour.

The Radar Operator:

Definition of "false positive": a test result that shows that something is there when, in reality, it is not.

This one seems to be fairly common, and could probably go on the chart as a Tier 4, if the woman crosses the line and becomes violent.

This type of *very* insecure woman always has her 'radar' going. No matter the time or place, it's always on—and it's *broken*. She doesn't understand that her radar keeps registering false positives.

She will zero-in on a woman down the block, around the corner and through the woods, if that woman even so much as *glances* in the direction of her man. That's when her radar (falsely) registers something moving into her airspace and she flips out.

"Was that woman staring at you? Don't act stupid; you saw her! Do you know her? Is there something I should know about? Did you date her? You *slept* with her, didn't you? Is that why she was looking at you? I'm going to have a little talk with that ho, *right now*! She is going to understand that I'm not going to have her staring at *my* man!"

If she's not going after some *woman*, for no real reason, she's going off on her man. If the man's eyes go anywhere near the direction of another woman, she thinks he's checking out another female.

"*Oh*. Um, e*xcuse* me. Were you checking her out? Don't you lie to me; I saw you cut your eyes! Did you like what you saw? Say it! Is that what you want? You want some little skank, like that?"

This type of crazy will make *you* crazy, since you are constantly stressed-out, having to calm her down and convince her that you don't want anyone else—and there *isn't* anyone else—in your life. Even though you are completely innocent, you're made to feel guilty, *all the time*, everywhere you go.

She's probably trying to get into your cellphone, to check your messages and call history, *right now*.

Forget lovemaking, and quality time together in public, in this type of marriage. There's no trust, whatsoever; there is only anger, resentment, distance and hurt. A relationship can very quickly, and easily, wither and die in this type of environment.

The Fragile Egg:

This is the relationship doom-and-gloom over-thinker. Even when things are going well, she will begin to think that maybe things are going *too* well, and that disaster is bound to happen.

She gets all up in her own headspace and begins to freak herself out—over *nothing*—always picking his words apart, looking for the negative in *everything*. She may otherwise be a great person, but leaving her with too much time to think about life and relationships can often lead her down a rabbit hole of darkness, and a coming relationship apocalypse.

The Good Guy will come home to a quiet house, and the *Fragile Egg* will be waiting for him—probably with alcohol in hand, having already had a couple of drinks (or five). As soon as the man sees her waiting, and notices that everything in the house is quiet, he will probably ask, "Hey, honey. Is everything okay?"

Oh, that poor soul! Why did he have to speak those mystical words and open a portal to the Crazy Dimension, right in his own living room?

When the portal is opened, the *Fragile Egg* will crack under the burst of power exploding into the room from the Crazy Dimension, and the evil Yoke of Doubt will come seeping out of her, all over the couch, the floor, the walls—and him.

She will question him on why he loves her in the first place, because she doesn't see herself as being good enough, beautiful enough, or smart enough, or some other insecurity, because bad things happened to her at some point in her life, and she's still carrying around the emotional baggage.

She walks around in a constant state of fear, waiting for (what she believes to be) the inevitable, and nothing he can say will make much difference. Even when he says something nice to reassure her, her brain twists it into something he did not intend, making it even worse!

As she is drowning in the yoke of her insecurities, the poor guy is now about to lose *his* mind, with constantly having to reassure her and keep himself from drowning in her muck.

He is about to claw his own eyes out, thinking that if she could just understand that he is with her because he loves her the way she is, and that it's impossible to be 100% perfect to all people—and that it's okay, because the definition of "perfect" is different for each person—things could be so much better! She is perfect for *him*, if only she could understand that, and love her wonderful self for who she truly is (which will also probably be twisted by her dark brain into something negative that he did not intend).

As she is sinking in the muck of doubt and despair, he reaches out a hand to her, to try to save her, but the Crazies on the other side of the dimensional wall keep whispering to her through the portal, "You know that it will all eventually end in heartbreak, anyway, so there's no need to fight for it and prolong the agony. Just sink, and let it end, now. He will never understand you the way *we* do."

He's thinking about walking out, because she's making the home a super-stressful madhouse!

The Tracker:

The Tracker has gone so far as to determine precisely how many miles your house is away from your usual destinations (work, grocery store, hobby shop, parents' house, etc.), and how much time it takes for you to get there. She monitors the time, and your car's odometer, to make sure you go where you say you're going, every time you leave your home.

She wants to know the name of the store you're in, when shopping at the local mall. She may send constant texts, or repeatedly call you, to get status updates when you're away. She may even go so far as to hide a GPS tracking device somewhere on your car, to keep tabs on you, in case you veer off of your typical path, because any deviation from the norm means that you are obviously a "CHEATER!"

Insecurity drives this type of woman to obsess over your location and activities, any time you are not in sight.

The Vampire:

Sadly, this woman's heart is ice-cold. Regardless of the reason for her transformation, she is a self-centered, unfeeling, disconnected and uncaring creature of darkness.

The *Vampire* seeks out, and preys upon, submissive men. She charms them, and then financially *drains* them. A man is basically food, and a means of survival, for her and her kids.

The *Vampire* often requires her (current) male submissive—and any others she may have, on the side—to hand over the paychecks. Her wrath will be swift and merciless when money is spent without her permission!

The man is required to spend most of his money on her, her home, her kids, and anything else she desires—and she will keep the man close to her, busy, and separated from family and friends, so that the people close to the man won't discover what is actually happening and try to interfere.

The *Vampire* is skilled in seduction, makes promises (lies), and gives just enough hot, physical affection—or the *promise* of such (another lie)—to keep the man hooked, but there is no love there. She may actually *despise* the man she is with, but she keeps him hooked until she can find a man who has more to offer. The sex—or *promise* of sex—is simply a means to an end.

When the man has outlived his usefulness to her, or broken her rules (refuses to submit), she has no problem with kicking the man out into the street, leaving him to fend for himself. She couldn't care less about what happens to him, because he didn't matter to her in the first place.

The Feral Cat

This type of woman is very similar to *The Vampire*, because they are both in survival mode, but the two types approach survival in different ways.

The Feral Cat is like the wild cat you sometimes see roaming through your backyard, as it's looking for food and places to hide. You call to it, but it freezes in place, stands defensively, stares at you for a split second, then runs away.

This type of woman may have abandonment issues, suffered great personal or financial loss, been betrayed on a deep level, or come from a dysfunctional family. Because of that, she has grown tough, streetwise, crafty, self-sufficient and *very* defensive. Her first instinct is to put a wall between her and anything that might cause her to compromise her defensive, self-reliant position.

The Feral Cat may have become friends—or at least given the *impression* that she is friends—with many people, because she is very well aware of the benefits that can come with maintaining connections to others who are strong, capable and willing to help her in times of want or need.

Sex can be good, but it's more for fun and physical release. It could also be the only way she knows of reaching out, or experiencing some level of connection—in a limited way, for a brief period of time. Even so, she may look at herself as being weak and compromising, or feel scared, after the fact—which also makes her want to run away, again.

This type of woman usually *wants* to love, and be loved, but she's too scared to trust, lower her defenses, and put faith in others, in order to get it. If she *does* find love, she may start to question it, feel overwhelmed by it, and eventually run from it, making things even worse for the future.

The Tier 3 Crazy may promise paradise, but she delivers a kiss of death!

Tier 4 Crazy: This woman's life is nothing but chaos, and she is out of control.

Mood swings are common. She's violent, especially when she's had a few drinks. She might key your car, or break things, in fits of anger or paranoia.

She's a disaster, maybe even a stalker, or someone who harms herself—or even a murder-suicide (you-her), waiting to happen.

If you want someone who can't separate dreams from reality—and might go nuts and stab you, while you sleep— this type may be your dream come true.

Tier 5 Crazy: This type of crazy is in a mental institution. She has completely lost her grasp of reality, and is no longer a functioning member of society.

❧

At this point in my life, a Tier 2 is what I want, but I think that actually *finding* a Tier 2 is going to be very difficult. They seem to be a rare breed, or I just haven't been looking in the right places. I haven't given up, though—at least, not yet.

If I do find one, and we connect, she's going to get all my love, attention and support. And I don't care who she is, or where she comes from; if she's the right woman for me, I'll cherish, love and protect her, until the end of my days.

❧

Please note: While this chapter, and much of this book, is written in a comical and sarcastic tone, I learned early in life that mental health is a very serious issue.

If you think you might need mental health assistance or emotional support, please don't hesitate to contact a licensed healthcare professional in your area. There is no shame in asking for help.

Also, speak to a local church pastor, or Christian friend, and seek support and guidance in asking God for healing and transformation.

Your health is important, and YOUR LIFE MATTERS!

CHAPTER 8

INTROVERTS & EXTROVERTS

A good number of Good Guy husbands I met over the years were on the introverted side, and it wasn't uncommon to see them pairing with women who were extroverted. I've also seen several examples of the opposite.

The problem comes with the extrovert getting their emotional 'batteries' *charged* by interacting with others, while the introvert's batteries are actually *drained* by interacting in social situations (parties, weddings, etc.). This can present problems in relationships, as you can probably guess.

If your man often has reservations about going out to mingle—especially with people he doesn't know very well—or often says he is ready to go home after being out for an hour or so, I wouldn't be surprised if you are dealing with an introvert.

I have been on both sides of this issue, so I will share some of my personal experiences.

Somewhere along the way in life, I became one of those "life of the party" guys. I'm not even sure how it happened, but at some point, in my young-adult life, I could walk into a local club and go to just about any table or group and turn up the energy level. I knew most of the people there, and we would have a blast all night long.

I never drank alcohol, smoked, or did any drugs—and still don't—but I absolutely loved to be around live music, get (reasonably) crazy with the guys, and flirt with the girls!

I eventually started seeing a girl who was really sweet and laid-back. I got out of the club scene, and tried to build a successful, satisfying relationship with her.

She was good to me, fun-loving, and had some of the prettiest eyes I had ever seen. We had some great times together, and I wanted things between us to work, but I was dealing with some issues that I just couldn't get past, so I eventually ended the relationship.

A whirlwind of a girl came into the picture, after that. We were only together a few months, but I was deeply affected by the breakup.

I think the fact that I had not been alone (without a girlfriend) for some time—combined with a lot of difficulties in my personal and business life—hit me extremely hard, and all of it took a very serious toll on me, all at once. It was one of those "when it rains, it pours" situations, so I basically went into survival mode.

Before that breakup, I was a happy-go-lucky kind of guy who could not wait to clock out of work at the end of the week, pack a weekend bag, drive out of town for a new adventure, hang out with my girl or some friends, and not come home until right before I had to be back at work. I was spontaneous, full of life, happy, and living a young man's "work hard, play hard" dream.

I was *very* extroverted, and being around other people, doing all kinds of fun things, charged my emotional batteries and left me wanting so much more. I never wanted a break in the action, and I was always disappointed if someone decided they wanted to go home and end the festivities.

After the breakup—and dealing with things that were beyond my control, in other areas of my life—my personality changed. I hit an emotional rock bottom, and I was all alone. My whole world had been turned upside-down, suddenly. I felt completely isolated, and was in a very dark place, for quite a while.

At some point, I decided to pick myself up and cut through the darkness. I got myself back in order, got tougher, more determined, restarted my career, and reintroduced humor and sarcasm into my life—but I was no longer extroverted.

I can go out with some friends, and have fun, but I'm not the "life of the party" kind of guy I used to be. I'm much more logical, grounded and even-keeled, now, and I don't like to stay in one place for long.

With a small group, it isn't bad, especially if I know them well, but with larger groups, and unfamiliar people, it doesn't usually take very long for me to feel drained and burned-out.

If I'm a manager on the job, I'm in manager mode, and have no problem taking control of a business situation. It's *socializing* that eventually drains my energy.

I want to stress that it usually has nothing to do with the people in the group; the problem is my brain telling me that it's simply had quite enough social stimulation, so I need to take it home. I used to be a crazy extrovert in public, but now I am clearly an observant introvert.

When one spouse is extroverted, and the other is not, the extrovert might feel that the introvert is just being petty, weak, afraid, controlling, or doesn't like the people in the group. With me, personally, that is not true, at all.

Speaking from personal experience, some introverts can't even explain exactly what it is they're feeling, or why they are feeling it; they simply feel a very strong urge to get away from all of the social stimulation—which can cause misunderstandings and arguments, especially if the extrovert wants to stay, disregarding the introvert's discomfort.

With me, when I feel it's time to go, it's because I feel emotionally and mentally drained; I'm simply out of energy. It's not a panic attack or anxiety; it's just a feeling of having expended all of my energy reserves, and I am *done*. I don't want to talk, anymore. I no longer want to hang out. I'm polite, and I love everyone, but I need to go and recharge. The longer I'm there, the worse I feel.

The key for couples is to acknowledge that it isn't (hopefully) just some ploy by your spouse to get out of going to your cousin's wedding, for example. This really is a thing. The challenge is to devise plans on how to make it work.

Making things work for the *both* of you may involve agreeing to do some things separately, or doing the activities that both of you want to do, together, but in shorter segments of time.

Instead of staying for an entire outdoor concert, with a group of friends, maybe just the two of you could go, and just for the time in which the band(s) you really want to see will be taking the stage. Also, maybe retreat to the lobby, or other open area, between bands. You can catch up with your friends, afterward, for a little afterparty.

Instead of spending all afternoon wandering around a shopping outlet, through the crowds of shoppers, take time to research the shops that are available and pick out the ones you both really want to visit. Speak to your spouse and agree on the amount of time to spend shopping, before you go.

If the introvert can go longer than expected, and is having a positive experience, *great!* If not, the extrovert could be a real hero by being understanding and considerate—which will lead to your introvert partner being more willing to try things, in the future, knowing that you respect them. They will begin to understand that they can count on you to not make them suffer when they feel that things are just too much to handle. (We all want to feel secure, right?)

If the extrovert feels absolutely bored out of their skull at the thought of going to a bookstore, a museum, a nighttime walk on the beach, or a movie, maybe the extrovert could give it a shot, once in a while, for a reasonable amount of time, just to be there for their spouse. In return, the introvert should try to make time to do something that charges the *extrovert's* batteries, too.

When it comes to introverts and extroverts, compromise and respect could go a long way to keeping both of you happy and fully engaged with each other.

CHAPTER 9

PLAYING HARD TO GET

This is more for the dating arena, but for many Good Guys, if you play "hard to get" with us, we assume you aren't interested. Again, we aren't mind readers, we don't want to seem pushy, or desperate, and we aren't good with hints, so we don't always see the game you're playing.

To be fair, some guys enjoy the chase. Personally, I do not, and neither do many of the Good Guys I've met.

If you're playing head games, guys like me see that as drama and control—and we *hate* that! We do understand that you want to feel desired, or that you might be trying to weed-out the persistent guys who just want no-strings sex, but there are better ways of getting what you want than toying around with us. (Believe it or not, guys want to feel desired, too!)

If you like the guy, talk to him and let him know you would like to spend time with him. With many Good Guys, if you try to play a game, we might just walk away (*I* would).

If he's truly a Good Guy, you won't have to worry about him being a jerk to you if he isn't interested in dating. If he *is* interested, then it was well worth it.

On the flip-side of that is a Good Guy simply being nice to you, and you getting the wrong idea.

Personally, I buy snacks and drinks, give helpful books, regularly make conversation with friends and coworkers, and enjoy helping the underdogs (I was one, too). Sometimes, people get the wrong idea, and mistake my being nice and generous for flirtation. Sorry, but that's not the case.

If a nice guy you know is always happy to help, regularly says hello, easily starts conversations with you, etc., it doesn't necessarily mean he's into you; a lot of Good Guys just enjoy being friendly and helpful to those around them. With a genuine Good Guy, it isn't some game; he's simply a nice man, plain and simple.

Personally, if I'm into a woman, I'm not afraid to tell her that I'm interested in getting to know her much better, once I feel that she and I are compatible. There will be no doubt, because I don't mind being straightforward. I can't stand it when people play games with me, so I won't play games with others.

If the woman is into me, too, great! We can take all the time we want in getting to know each other better, to see where things can go from there, once we've determined that there's mutual attraction. If she's *not* into me, I've saved myself a lot of time and effort.

CHAPTER 10

PAWNS IN RELATIONSHIP GAMES

Please, *never* use your kids as pawns in twisted, confrontational games with your spouse. Don't even *think* about it. Not only will your spouse probably never forgive you for it, but you could also scar your children for life by using them as pawns in a sick game. Your children, too, may never forgive you for it, once they reach sufficient age to understand how you tried to use them.

Telling children lies about their mom or dad, to get revenge because you're mad about something, is child abuse, in my view. Just because you may be angry in the moment, or actually separating from your spouse, don't deny the love and attention that children need and want from *both* parents.

You can still be unhappy with each other—and settle your personal business, privately—but, please, don't put your kids in the middle of it.

If there's a possibility of harm and abuse, that's one thing; children should always be kept safe and secure. It's a different ballgame, altogether, to attempt to get your children to believe that your spouse is a bad person, simply because you're having another disagreement, and you play dirty to "win."

CHAPTER 11

EGOS ARE KILLING YOUR RELATIONSHIP

Personally, I have never seen a relationship that did not eventually have some level of conflict, misunderstanding, or disagreement. The stable marriages I have witnessed involved a husband and wife who learned how to navigate those conflicts, and preserve the peace, while resolving their issues.

Successful partners learn to put their egos aside and willingly listen, admit mistakes, apologize, ask for forgiveness, openly and honestly communicate, change behaviors that negatively impact their spouse, put their sincere love for each other into action, are open to suggestion and compromise, and remain respectful.

You can constantly fight about who is to blame, and "win" every argument, but you'll eventually *lose* your relationship, if fighting to win and be "right" is all you ever do.

I'm very happy with who I am—independent and very individualistic—but I also have massive amounts of love for a woman with whom I'm in a positive relationship. Because of that, I'm willing to work on a lot of things in marriage—as long as I am not being pushed to become someone completely different (more on that, later).

CHAPTER 12

ACT YOUR AGE! (AND DIE AN EARLY DEATH!)

Is there an official chart that details exactly what you're supposed to be doing, and how you're supposed to be acting, at every age? If so, I haven't found it—and I wouldn't care to look at it, if I did!

Personally, I find "acting your age" to be ridiculous and subjective—and potentially dangerous for your health. It also smacks of jealousy and control issues.

Doing things that I enjoy, and spending time with others who have a similar outlook on life, makes me happier and healthier. I feel that it's definitely better to laugh and enjoy good, clean fun than it is to be worried about what other people might say about it.

If you like to dance in the rain, or go to costume parties, go right ahead!

Maybe you enjoy playing wacky golf, or completing puzzles on the kitchen table. Rock on!

Video games? Knock yourself out!

Do you enjoy fishing, or other outdoor activities? More power to you!

Are you a fan of board games, or card games, and enjoy having weekly game nights at home or the hobby store? Cool!

Do you have a collection of baby dolls on the shelf? I know absolutely *nothing* about doll collecting, but if it makes you happy then go for it!

Maybe you like to go crazy with Christmas decorations. If so, have fun!

Do you enjoy rock concerts? Let's go!

Still play role-playing games? I do, too! Let's start a new campaign!

I'm very young at heart, and enjoy fun times, so I want to surround myself with people who enjoy life.

Age doesn't make a lot of difference to me, as long as you're an adult, mature, respectful, responsible, you bring something positive to our friendship, and you enjoy good and wholesome things. I've encountered good and bad in every age category, so I am much more concerned with the quality of a person's character, these days.

I have mostly younger friends, because most people my age seem to act. . .well, *old*. Sadly, they let their *age* define who they are, and what they will allow themselves to enjoy.

If they have physical ailments that hinder them from engaging in certain activities, that's a different matter, and I completely understand. If they refuse to have some good, clean fun, because they're worried about what someone else will say about it, I find that to be ridiculous.

I hear "I'm way too old for that" (you're not!), "That's for the younger folks" (it's for *anyone!*), "I would look silly doing that" (who cares?), or "That music is too loud!" (okay, you're too old).

My younger friends and I enjoy many of the same activities, music, games, movies, books, etc. If I was hung up on age, or the activities we could enjoy, I would have missed out on some great times and great people.

I do have some wonderful friends that are my age and older, and they usually bring something different to the table, as far as wisdom, stability, accountability, life experiences and perspective are concerned. It's not the same dynamic, but I value *all* of the people I call "friend," regardless of their age.

Just remember that other people don't have to live your life, and they don't have to live with the decisions you make for yourself. Relax and enjoy the good things that make you happy—and don't worry too much about whether or not some fuddy-duddy neighbor down the street thinks you aren't "acting your age."

CHAPTER 13

A **REAL** MAN

We are all different, and have our own strengths and weaknesses. There is no cookie-cutter mold that a male has to fit into, in order to be a "*real* man." Men come from all types of backgrounds, races, personalities, body types and skill sets.

Celebrate, and utilize, the wonderful gifts with which you and your Good Guy husband are blessed. Don't harp on the shortcomings, or those things that are not in the nature of some men—unless you actually enjoy arguments and hurting your husband. Don't be that kind of wife: the *divorced* kind.

There's a nasty, ridiculous old saying about a woman's place being in the kitchen and the bedroom. It's infuriating and insulting, right? Yes, it is! And a *man's* place isn't in the *garage* or the *toolshed*, either!

But could your Good Guy husband give something a fair try, before dismissing it? Absolutely, but the chance of success will depend on his skills, knowledge, abilities, and the particular situation.

Just always remember one *very* important thing: If your Good Guy doesn't succeed, never make him feel like he's less of a man, or a failure, just because he isn't skilled in a certain area, or he's physically incapable of getting a certain job done.

Work on things that are more comfortable for him (within his area of skill and physical abilities), first, and get some successes under the belt, before attempting more complicated, difficult and unfamiliar tasks. Success breeds confidence—and often more willingness to tackle new things in the future.

Also, I hear "She's trying to change me into someone else!" from Good Guy husbands who feel that their wives are trying to push them into being different people, altogether. I've seen just about everything, from trying to change a man's wardrobe, hairstyle, car, routine, hobbies, friends—even food preferences.

Don't turn your husband into a project—something to be molded and manipulated into your self-centered idea of who he should be. Having goals, and helping each other become better people can be a positive thing, but trying to completely remake someone into your preferred image is not.

For those still in the dating stage, do your homework *before* you commit to a serious relationship or marriage. Be honest with yourself about what you need and desire in a man, or you could end up with a lot of regret and wasted time.

Guys, this goes for you, too, when it comes to finding the right woman.

CHAPTER 14

EYE OF THE BEHOLDER

I was in a retail store, having a conversation with one of my female friends, when she pointed out a young woman who was wearing a very sexy outfit. As we began talking about obvious attempts to get attention, by wearing revealing clothing, my friend asked, "But don't you want other people to think that your girlfriend or wife is hot and attractive?"

Immediately, I replied, "Honestly, I don't care what other people think. If we love and adore each other, and we're happy, that's all that matters to me; I don't need the approval of others. If other people think she's pretty, that's great—and I do want her to feel pretty, because she certainly is—but she's beautiful to *me*, regardless of what anyone else has to say about it."

I added, "I would prefer her to be viewed and respected as a classy lady, in public, but be as free and uninhibited with me, in the privacy of our home, as she wants to be. I feel that some things are sacred, and only for our spouses, as a private and personal pleasure that we only share with each other—including showing off our bodies."

Maybe your spouse feels the same way.

CHAPTER 15

THE TOUGH QUESTIONS

This is for people who are still in the dating pool.
At an appropriate point in your relationship, you may
want to ask certain questions, discuss the answers, and
get a few things out in the open, to determine if you're
both truly compatible. Pay attention to the answers given,
because they can reveal a lot about a person.

Some questions are more appropriate to ask after a
committed relationship has been established, but there are
some questions that I would definitely ask on a first date,
to determine compatibility (I don't want to waste time or
effort on something that is never going to work). You will
have to be the judge and determine the proper time to ask
each one.

Examples:

"What type of relationship are you looking for?"

"What is your idea of the perfect date?"

"What one thing could someone do for you that would
make you feel like the most-loved person on the planet?"

"If you knew that the world was going to end in
twenty-four hours, how would you want to spend that
remaining time?"

"Do you want children? If so, how many?"

"What are your views, when it comes to disciplining
children?"

"Do you consider yourself to be a liberal, conservative, libertarian, communist, anarchist, voluntaryist, or something else, altogether?" (Definitely, a first date question, for me!)

"What are your views on taxation?" (The only acceptable answer: "Taxation is *theft!*")

"Are you a Christian? If so, what denomination? Do you regularly attend church?"

"How serious are you about your Christian Faith?"

"Do you feel that we should pool money together, and have an account just for bills, or keep separate bank accounts and divide the bills between us?"

"What hobbies and outside activities are most important to you? How often do you enjoy doing them?"

"How do you feel about having close friends of the opposite sex? What types of boundaries would you expect?"

"What are some of your pet peeves?"

"Would you want our kids to attend public or private school, or be homeschooled?"

"Do you have a favorite charity that you support?"

"Would you want a dog, a cat, or some other animal— or no pets, at all?"

"Where do you see us in 5 years?"

"What are your career plans?"

"Do you have a good relationship with your parents?"

"What is your current financial situation?"
"Do you eat meat?"

"Are you pro-choice or pro-life, when it comes to abortion?

"How do you feel about keeping firearms in the home, for protection—and for fun at the shooting range?"

"Do you feel that lovemaking is important to the health of a good marriage?"

"Are you currently being treated for any physical, mental or emotional condition?"

"Do you believe in man-made climate change?" (Answer: "No! That's politically-motivated nonsense.")

There are more that could be asked, of course, but that's a good start.

CHAPTER 16

FAKEUP

Women can get facelifts, toxic injections, tummy tucks, fake boobs, fake buns, eyelashes, fingernails, hair, hair color, teeth, and even eye color.

They can use push-up bras, padded bras, cleavage-enhancing bras, stick-on bras, eyelash curlers, tweezers, mascara, eyeliner, eye shadow, styling gels, curlers, blush, straighteners, mousse, volumizers, lip gloss, breast tape, hairspray, "tummy control" underwear, "plumping" makeup and serums, blemish cream, foundation, *concealer* (the name, alone, says it all), and more, to become someone completely different than they really are, yet I hear some of them say that they are tired of "fake men," and yearn for an "honest man."

Yeah. Let that sink in for a moment.

I know what women are talking about when they mention "fake men," but if we're going to talk about people being fake, let's include the way many *men* feel about fake *women*, too—like how some women flirt with men at a bar, just to get free drinks, knowing they aren't interested in the men, right from the start. (I hate to be the one to break it to you, sweetheart, but that's being fake, too.)

Personally, I'm turned off by false eyelashes, red lipstick and red nail polish; those things just scream "fake!" to me, because they look so unnatural. I like it much better when a woman uses makeup to lightly enhance the beautiful features she already possesses—instead of being someone I wouldn't recognize after the makeup is washed off, and all of the accessories, attachments and props are removed.

CHAPTER 17

CONNECTIONS

Generally speaking, a man feels more connected to his wife when he is engaged in physical contact with her.

A woman is more open to engaging in physical contact with her husband when she feels more emotionally connected to him through non-sexual interaction and communication—and both of those connections are *equally* valid and important. The problem is often where to start, along this vicious circle, to get to a point where husband and wife both feel connected to each other *at the same time*.

For a woman, foreplay often begins in her *mind*, with conversation, undivided attention, and the sharing of personal and intimate details of life. For a man, foreplay often begins with a look of desire and a soft touch—or his lovely wife whispering something sexy in his ear.

Sexual intimacy goes to the very core of many men, because it plays a big part in feelings of self-worth, deeper emotional connection and masculinity. If the wife rejects her husband's touch, the husband often wonders if he has done something wrong, if he is inadequate, undesirable, or his wife no longer loves him—or maybe his wife is having an affair with someone she *does* find desirable. Rejection of his touch feels like a rejection of *him*, because many men feel that their sexuality is a very significant and defining aspect of who they are. With some men, rejection can feel like an emotional castration, but sexual intimacy is total acceptance—acceptance of him, his love, his body, his very *essence*.

A lot of hurt, frustration and division could be avoided, and your relationship strengthened, by working to fulfill each other's physical and emotional needs, more often.

Ladies, if you want your Good Guy husband to be more emotionally connected to you, try to be positive, enthusiastic, and sincerely engaged in the moment, when he wants to physically connect with you—even if you've had a disagreement. I know that sounds a little crazy, but hear me out on this one.

Have you ever had a fight, gone to bed, rolled over with your back toward your husband, and then felt him attempt to touch your arm, put his arm around you, caress your back, or kiss your shoulder? You probably wondered how he could even *think* about touching you when you're still upset, right?

Remember, for many men, a *physical* connection is how they express and experience love, so when your husband reaches out to you through touch it's his way of attempting to overcome the negativity and re-establish a loving, emotional connection with you. He wants some reassurance, and to feel safe, knowing that you are still willing to accept his love, and show him love in return, even if you're currently frustrated or angry with him.

Believe me, we know what we are risking by attempting to touch you when you're angry, so we aren't doing it just to try to get laid!

Instead of rejecting him, try making an effort to reconnect with him in *his* way. It doesn't have to lead to lovemaking—though it *could*, if you both decide you want to feel that kind of closeness in the moment, and use it to re-establish a very intimate connection to each other.

A loving touch has a way of soothing, calming and reassuring. You may find the emotional connection that *you* want returns, too—even if you're still a bit upset—and that things are much easier to resolve when you are calmer, more connected and less adversarial. It's a good time to put your egos aside, calm down, hold each other, apologize to each other, *forgive* each other, and talk, if nothing else, because your husband is reaching out, in his own way, wanting peace and *connection* with you.

Men, if you want to be more *physically* connected, be available for your wife when she wants to connect with you on her type of emotional level—which includes sincere, meaningful conversation, and regularly spending *non-sexual*, quality time together.

An emotional connection with you is *extremely* important to your wife, and it is the foundation upon which everything else in your marriage will rest. If it isn't strong, your relationship could eventually crumble and fall.

Your wife wants to know that you are both on the same page in life, that your relationship is solid and *secure*, and that you will always be there for her. She wants to know that you truly *value* her and how she feels, and that she can be completely vulnerable—but totally *safe*—in opening up and sharing deeply personal things with you.

She doesn't necessarily want you to "fix" anything; often, she just wants you to be a good listener, supporter and comforter.

Be genuine and thoughtful when listening to her, and provide security by being the man in her life that she can always count on. Do these things, and you will probably notice a change in how much more receptive she is to your touch—and how much more often *she* initiates the physical contact and connection that *you* need.

Connect with the *mind*, and the body will follow—and when it does, she's probably going to want and need a lot of physical foreplay, so don't rush it! Men can spring to attention, and be ready for lovemaking, in a matter of seconds. Most women, on the other hand, need some time to warm up and properly prepare their bodies for lovemaking.

If your wife doesn't have sufficient time to naturally lubricate, loosen up her vaginal tissues and get increased blood flow going to her clitoris, lovemaking for her can be very uncomfortable—or even *painful*—so take the time to make sure that your wife is ready. (Get a clue: People seek out things that feel good, but *avoid* things that do not.)

I'm including this silly—but ultimately serious—analogy, because I'm sad to say that many men just don't get it, when it comes to the importance of foreplay: Husband, think of your wife as a charcoal grill. That's right, a grill.

1) **She needs you to ignite her flame** (talk with her, spend non-sexual, quality time with her, and sincerely connect, emotionally, first); 2) **let the flames burn for a while and spread** (lots of kissing, caressing, holding each other, sensually massaging, and other uses of hands and mouths that get you both highly aroused); 3) **cook only when the coals are perfect** (wait until she is very turned on and desiring passionate lovemaking). **And don't rush *any* of it!**

You probably know what it takes to get the grill ready for cooking. Make sure you get your *wife* ready, too, before making love, for a much better experience—for *both* of you.

In the bedroom, become a servant to your wonderful queen. Put her needs above yours, and make sure she feels loved, important, cared for, completely safe and satisfied.

Enjoy touching, caressing and exploring her soft, beautiful body. Pay attention to her movements, and listen to the sounds of approval that she makes as you are pleasing her.

Take care of *her* needs—*first*—the same way you want her to take care of *your* needs, and you may notice an increase in the quality, and frequency, of your lovemaking.

One more thing: Show your spouse some respect and TAKE A SHOWER—and that goes for *both* of you! It's especially important to be clean and fresh before sexual intimacy. I personally don't know of anyone who wants a sticky, smelly, greasy, dirty, germy person in bed with them.

Your spouse probably isn't going to want to touch you—or do anything *else* to you—if you are offensive in smell and taste, so find a natural body wash or soap that cleans away all the funk, while leaving you with a light, pleasant scent.

Better yet, take a shower *together* and soap each other up. Turn getting clean into hot foreplay. Just make sure you are truly washed and clean, before you rush to towel off and jump into bed together!

Alternatively, if you have a large bathtub, prepare a warm bubble bath. Light some candles, bring a small tray of fruit pieces or other light snacks. Feed each other, and enjoy taking your time to clean and caress each other, in a relaxed way.

When you make the effort to clean yourself, you show that you care about your spouse's comfort level and health.

CHAPTER 18

"SIT. ROLL OVER. PLAY DEAD. GOOD BOY!"

Having serious relationship conflict, and not feeling the desire for sexual intimacy, because of drama and turmoil, is understandable. Using sex to manipulate or control someone is another matter, altogether.

If your Good Guy husband has to jump through hoops, and obey your commands and demands before you will allow him to touch you, I feel that you are treating him like a dog who is performing for treats and pats on the head. He's not a dog, so don't treat him like one!

Withholding sexual intimacy in that manner is nothing more than a power trip, and a very nasty head game that can cause serious problems within a relationship. Your husband may even get to a point where he no longer feels the struggle is worth it, and may lose his desire to be with you—or be *around* you. When it gets to that point, your relationship is in serious trouble.

Regular lovemaking can reportedly strengthen bonds of trust and intimacy between husband and wife, and I have heard health professionals refer to regular lovemaking as being "glue" that helps to hold marriages together.

The "7 Day Sex Challenge" has been around for many years, and there are a lot of online videos made by married couples who took the week-long challenge and reported great results. There was even a reality TV series that featured couples on the brink of divorce who turned their marriages around after taking the challenge—and all it took was seven consecutive nights of lovemaking, regardless of their moods and attitudes, to get them moving in the right direction.

Many health organizations and health news websites have stated that lovemaking can lower stress levels, elevate your mood, boost brain power, ease the pain of arthritis, boost your immune system, stop migraines, improve sleep, improve hair and skin quality, improve your sense of smell, reduce the risk of heart disease and prostate cancer, lower blood pressure, and more. Semen has also been shown to be an anti-depressant, for women.

Making love is healthy. Treating your husband like a dog is not.

While we are on the subject of making love, there are other behaviors that kill sexual desire in many Good Guy husbands.

Do you feel the need to make your husband understand how you feel about something he's done that you didn't like, or something he didn't do that you wanted him to do, right before the two of you start fooling around—literally, right before the touching and kissing starts?

Do you show your displeasure, and disconnect from him, by acting distant, having a negative attitude, or not getting into it while in bed together?

Are you trying to send a message, hoping that he will get the hint and ask you if something's wrong—or sabotaging the moment, in order to justify feelings of low self-esteem—effectively ruining the experience, and turning your bed into a negative space? If you are, you are probably killing his desire to get close to you, or initiate contact! (If you said "Good!" I am *very* concerned for the future of your marriage.)

What man wants to get all worked up, thinking he's going to make love to his beautiful, amazing wife, only to realize that she wants to talk (beat him down, or criticize him), first, about how he's been screwing everything up?

If you want to destroy your husband's desire to connect with you, on any meaningful level, do those very things and you might get your wish—and maybe even a divorce.

Your Good Guy husband is being conditioned to feel that every time you two attempt to make love, he is going to have to sit through a long, libido-killing lecture that will probably end up in a fight, or him having to hold his tongue to keep the peace. Either way, some men feel it just isn't worth it.

I also realize that some of you might think that this is an effective way to make your husband feel some of the frustration or anger that *you've* been feeling. Sorry, but men and women feel things differently.

Good Guys usually don't like confrontation with their wives—and certainly don't like drama! Eventually, they will most likely withdraw, become distant, and spend more time with work, friends and hobbies.

If you have something you need to get out in the open and discuss with your husband, do it when you are not in bed and not about to make love! Make your bed a place for *positive* things—sleep, making love, relaxing, healing—*only*. Sexual intimacy is not a reward; it is extremely important for many men, because it is the way they connect. It shouldn't be used as a way to capture your audience for a tongue-lashing.

In my opinion, making love should be treated as a sacred, guilt-free, uninhibited, trust-promoting, healthy, necessary bonding experience between husband and wife. I feel that it plays a huge role in keeping marriages healthy.

After all of the stress and exhaustion from work, kids, bills, family issues, health concerns—really, any number of things that powerfully impact our lives on a daily basis—taking time to physically connect, bond, relax and unwind with your spouse is vitally important. Making it fun and thrilling is an added bonus! Attaching negative emotions to it can absolutely *destroy* it.

If you feel the need to have a discussion about things that are bothering you, schedule some time, so you both can talk—and you both know what is coming. Go for a walk, or a drive. Take it to some neutral area and work it out, and never do it in public. Whatever you do, keep it out of your *bedroom*! When you both go to bed, it should generate *positive* feelings and anticipation for love and connection.

Don't bring your *phone* to bed, either! Instead, talk, snuggle, make love, laugh, read a book together, listen to music, do crossword puzzles together—whatever makes you both happy. Keep things that distract you, or *separate* you, away from your bed. Use your bed to connect with each other, on some level, before sleep—and never forget to say, "I love you." (Go ahead and say it to your spouse, right now.)

CHAPTER 19

FALL IN LOVE AGAIN

After the honeymoon phase wears off, sometimes passion and romance can taper off, too. Husbands and wives often slip into comfort zones and predictable routines, while taking each other for granted.

While it was once very important to go out on dates, enjoy spending quality time together, and get dressed to impress each other, those things can become less and less of a priority, as bills, work schedules, family drama, and other sources of stress creep in and sap the energy out of a marriage. Before long, a couple can develop what I call Sweatpants & Boxers Syndrome (SBS).

Some symptoms of SBS: sweatpants or boxers are the typical choice of around-the-house attire; one or both spouses regularly fall asleep while watching TV; lovemaking doesn't happen very often; romance is nonexistent; husband and wife spend most of their time in different parts of the house, away from each other; meaningful conversation is a thing of the past; and, after a while, the man and woman end up living more like roommates than a married couple.

As I've said, everything is a choice, so *choose* to reconnect, fall in love again, and spend some wonderful time together.

The first move is often the hardest—because there may be some feelings of awkwardness, embarrassment, doubt, bitterness, etc.—but once you *choose* to push it aside, and move past it, your relationship could take a positive turn. It may not happen overnight, but at least you're moving in the right direction. With time and effort, you could be on your way to turning things around.

Date nights can be lifesavers in a marriage, too. Getting away from work, kids, in-laws, parents, neighbors, routines—and the home environment, itself—can be a real pick-me-up for your relationship. Whatever you decide to do, have *fun*, and reconnect in the ways that *both* of you need.

Try to find time, at least once a week, to disconnect from *everything* and focus solely on each other. Take turns choosing the activities, so both of you get to plan things that you will enjoy—or use the time to experience completely new things.

Go out, have a blast, laugh, be silly, hold hands, flirt with each other, hug, smile, walk arm in arm, kiss, and do the kinds of things that you used to do that made your spouse feel special, when you were just dating—those "Aww, that was so sweet!" moments. Bring the romance back, dress nicely for each other, and once in a while, if you're able, pack a bag and go away together for the weekend.

Turn your electronic devices off, and talk to each other the way you used to when you were dating. Discuss life, dreams, and what you love so much about each other.

If you can't always go out, let someone else keep the kids for the night, and plan for a romantic evening at home. Whip up a light, home-cooked meal, *together.* Snuggle on the couch. Watch a movie, and fall asleep in each other's arms, for example.

The key to making a connection with your spouse is to put the main focus on *each other*, not the activity. If you go into it with the mindset that this is about enjoying each other's company, it can be a big win for your relationship—and you'll still be able to laugh about it, and connect, even if the chosen activity falls flat, or doesn't work out the way you had hoped. (The activity isn't as important as the *connection* and time spent together.)

Keeping those emotional and physical connections alive and well can greatly increase happiness, and strengthen your marriage against outside forces that might try to tear it apart.

Take a moment to schedule a date night with your spouse, for next week (yes, *right now!*). Flirt with each other about it, and build anticipation all week long. I have no doubt that you'll be glad you did.

CHAPTER 20

SEX AND THE CHURCH

In many churches and religious households, sex and even marital lovemaking are taboo subjects.

Youth coming up in the church are told to guard their "private parts," because all of that sex stuff is "of the Devil!" Then when the youth get a little older, and marry, the newlyweds are expected to fumble through everything, and rewire their brains to be able to derive pleasure from being touched in those "private" places—without feeling guilty, or sinful, for making love to their spouse.

Yes, we should *always* work to keep the youth safe, and educate them on the sin of premarital sex. We should also go about teaching abstinence until marriage in a much better way, so that people understand that God intended something very different for *marriage*—the appropriate environment for sexual intimacy.

Our bodies, how they fit together, how we procreate, and how we enjoy the pleasure derived from it was all created by *God*, and it's a wonderful *gift* from God, to be fully enjoyed within the boundaries of monogamous marriage. Satan had absolutely *nothing* to do with our creation and physical design, but he has worked overtime to corrupt and destroy something that can be so vital to a healthy marriage—and I feel it's time that married Christians turned that around!

Some churches and parents teach that intercourse, for anything other than making babies, is sinful (the Bible says to be fruitful and multiply, but it doesn't say that you have to try to multiply every time you make love!), or that sex is a duty that wives should begrudgingly perform just to keep their husbands happy—which absolutely blows my mind! That type of incorrect instruction can cause a *lot* of problems in a marriage, and it's not even close to what God intended.

To be clear: *Premarital* sex is a sin, but lovemaking in marriage is meant to be pleasurable and satisfying, for both husband *and* wife. 1 Corinthians 7:3-5 basically says that lovemaking should also occur regularly, with husbands and wives being instructed to give authority over their bodies to each other, and not deny sexual relations, in order to lessen the threat from outside temptation.

Don't misunderstand; the verses in 1 Corinthians aren't meant to be used as a weapon, to push, guilt-trip or force your spouse into unwanted sexual relations with you. Sexual intimacy in marriage is supposed to be a positive and pleasurable experience that brings you *closer* together, not farther apart. Both of you should be working hard to get to a place in your marriage where your spouse's desire to be sexually intimate with you is *welcome*, and you look forward to the connection that you will share together.

If you have never read Song of Solomon (a.k.a. Song of Songs) in the Holy Bible, I recommend taking a look. It is a beautiful, metaphorical, poetic, erotic love story about sexual desire and pleasure. In it, the *woman* is desiring and pursuing, just as much as the man. (If you really want to go deep, check out Song of Solomon 2:3 and 4:16, in particular.)

Some pastors say that they have never preached a single sermon based on Song of Solomon, which is sad, considering how important lovemaking can be for marriage health.

I have personally researched, and asked a few Christian leaders that I respect, about biblical restrictions on marital sexual activity, and their opinions seem to agree with mine: There are no restrictions listed in the Bible that govern sexual activity between a loving, monogamous husband and wife.

Marital lovemaking is supposed to be uplifting, pleasurable and bond-strengthening, so negativity, force, abuse, exploitation, hurt, guilt or insecurity should never be a part of it. God never intended any marital sexual activity to be harmful or hurtful to you, your spouse or your relationship.

CHAPTER 21

NEEDS AND DESIRES

Each person has a lovemaking style that brings them the greatest level of satisfaction. Knowing your own, and your partner's—and openly and honestly sharing those desires—can make a *huge* difference in the level of sexual satisfaction within your marriage.

For example, some people like being tied up or restrained. Some folks want their lovemaking to be a soft and sensual "slow burn." Others like to be adventurous. Some couples like to role-play. Sex toys are a regular part of sexual fun for some couples. Sometimes, couples just want to rip off their clothes and go at it, fast and furiously. No matter how you prefer to make love, take time to *honestly and openly* share your needs and desires with your spouse.

Most Good Guys I've known are very eager to please, and get excited when their wife wants to initiate physical contact or try something new—and they want to be shown the same level of respect and consideration when they have something new that *they* want to try.

As I previously mentioned, in what I have researched in my Christian Faith, I believe that nothing is out-of-bounds in marriage, as long as it brings you closer together, doesn't involve anyone other than your spouse, and isn't harmful, hurtful, forced, disrespectful—you get the idea. You will have to decide what is and is not acceptable in your own marriage, but I would suggest that you keep an open mind and try to accommodate each other's preferences, when possible—but also be understanding and respectful if there is something your spouse doesn't feel comfortable doing.

Sexual frustration can be a relationship killer, so put effort into creating a non-judgmental, safe, private, respectful environment in which you can enjoy each other, try new things, and strengthen your connection.

CHAPTER 22

LOVE CONNECTION

If your child doesn't like coloring books, you might give him some modeling clay. If he doesn't like modeling clay, how about a model car? If his face lights up, he jumps for joy, and screams "You're the best mom, ever!" you make sure to add model cars to your gift list for that child, from now on, because you want him to be happy and feel loved.

If you learn that your cat loves to play with yarn, you give your cat a piece of yarn, because you love her and want her to be happy.

If you discover that your dog loves to play fetch, you play fetch with your dog, because you love him and want him to be happy.

Learning what makes your *spouse* feel loved and happy should be the most important thing of all!

The way in which your spouse needs to feel love from you may be different from the way that *you* need to feel love, but it is so vitally important to give love to him in *his* way, so that he knows, beyond any doubt, that he is truly loved and valued by you.

What is it that makes you feel the greatest love for, and connection to, your husband?

Do you feel the most loved when he paints the house, organizes the garage, or washes the dishes?

Do you feel the most loved when you are cuddling, kissing, hugging, holding hands or making love?

How about when you two are spending the day together, going to a museum, shopping, attending a rock concert or sporting event, or enjoying a great conversation over dinner at a nice restaurant?

Does it make you feel warm and fuzzy inside when your husband tells you that he is so incredibly proud of your hard work and accomplishments on the job, or the amazing things you do in your home to keep the family happy and healthy?

Are you a sapiosexual, a person who is primarily attracted to people who possess high levels of intelligence? If so, visiting an historic library with your spouse, or engaging in deep philosophical discussions, might trip your trigger.

Maybe your heart flutters when your husband comes home with a special gift that he put a lot of thought into. (Suggestions: favorite perfume, flowers, restaurant, clothing brand, hobby, candy, music, etc.)

And what about your husband? Do you know what makes *him* feel most loved and connected to you?

Determining how each of you feels and receives love is vital to the health of your relationship.

Most people seem to think that just because they feel love a certain way, that's how everyone *else* will feel love, too.

For example, if you feel most loved when someone gives you a thoughtful gift, you probably have a natural tendency to give gifts, thinking that surely others will feel loved by it. Sorry, but that isn't necessarily the case.

Believe it or not, some people just aren't turned on by gift-giving. In fact, some people feel funny about accepting gifts from others, for any number of reasons.

The point is that just because *you* feel loved in a certain way, it doesn't mean that others will feel it the same way that you do.

The trick is finding out what makes you both feel loved, and then giving those things to each other, regularly. Both of you should do them for each other—and the sooner you discover what those special things are, the better!

For kicks and giggles, let's say that you feel most loved when your husband tells you how proud he is of you and what you've accomplished in your professional career, and how you take such good care of the family. He loves and supports you, he frequently, lovingly brags on you, and says that he is lucky to have you.

If your husband brings flowers home to you, it's a very nice gesture, and you may think he's being sweet for doing so, but it doesn't trip your *love* trigger if you crave his support and encouragement, as in the above example. It's his words of undying support, how proud he is of you, and knowing that he stands behind you that fills your heart with love and affection for him.

If, in the support example, that's the way you feel the most loved, your husband should be giving you just that: Uplifting, encouraging support, and letting you know just how happy he is that you are his incredible, talented, hardworking, intelligent, beautiful wife.

Regarding your husband, you may truly enjoy making love with him, even though it isn't the way you feel most loved. Because you know that your *husband* feels most loved when you physically connect with him, you are happy to bond with him on that level, so he knows that you truly love him and are sensitive to how he needs to feel love from you.

Your husband may genuinely appreciate it when you give him your support and encouragement when he has to tackle a tough situation, but he may not feel the most loved in that way—*you* do, as in the previous example, but not him. Your words of support are nice, and he's very glad that you care, but he still doesn't truly feel *loved* in that way, though you feel that he should.

And while most men seem to feel a connection through physical touch, there are men who feel most loved in other ways, so don't assume that just giving your man a good "roll in the hay" will give him what he needs.

When it comes down to it, both of you should regularly work to give your spouse love in the way that they *need* it. Other ways of showing love and affection are very nice and appreciated, but nothing can take the place of what your spouse *needs* to feel from you.

Sit down and talk about it, even if you think you know the answers. Be completely honest and non-judgmental with each other about what you need, and leave no doubt.

Taking time to get to know these things about each other—and then making a regular habit of doing them—can work wonders in your marriage.

CHAPTER 23

MEN ARE VISUAL CREATURES

L adies, a man's brain is wired to look for physically-healthy, attractive females, for the purpose of creating strong, healthy, attractive offspring who will be better able to continue the man's genetic code and bloodline. This means that guys easily and instantly notice physical attributes—without even consciously thinking about it, usually—because it's just automatic.

Yes, even our Good Guy eyes will notice an attractive woman, but that doesn't mean that we are lusting after her and want to sex her up; it just means that we easily spot the things that we have been *genetically programmed* to notice.

Almost like a robotic scanner system, we do a split-second, subconscious assessment of all women that we view, and our brains will affirm when an attractive female walks past. We are highly visually stimulated, so, yeah, we notice—then it's quickly over, and we move right along. No harm, no foul. Please, don't get bent out of shape about it.

Our brains view the female form as God's ultimate work of art, and we basically walk through life's art gallery every day. But please understand that while we may appreciate the artwork, it doesn't mean that we want to 'nail' one to a wall!

It's kind of like the way you size-up other women that you meet. You notice each other's hairstyles, jewelry, purses, fingernails, brand names of clothes and accessories, even body shape and attributes—and God help us if two of you wear the exact same outfit to the same party!

You notice those kinds of things, too, when it comes to men.

You notice when a handsome man walks into the room—along with the nice watch, suit, tie, lady-killer smile, broad shoulders, facial hair, height, hairstyle and shoes he's wearing. He is attractive, but (hopefully) it doesn't mean you want to run over and jump his bones. It's the same with Good Guys, when it comes to women, and not a big deal—as long as it's just very brief, innocent recognition, and absent of lust.

Noticing something, and *lusting* after something, are two very different things, in my opinion. If you're lusting after someone other than your spouse (which the Bible says is also adultery), pray for strength, forgiveness and a change of heart—and if you feel you may lack the inner strength to overcome certain temptations, don't put yourself in situations where you might be tempted by them!

CHAPTER 24

"MEN WILL HAVE SEX WITH <u>ANYTHING!</u>"

While there are indeed some men who will tap anything with a hole and a heartbeat, the Good Guys I've known would not, so I disagree with that stereotype.

When I was a young, single, naughty, long-haired rocker, I usually enjoyed the opportunity to fool around with a pretty girl, but I did turn it down on several occasions—especially if I knew I'd have to deal with a guilty conscience, the next day.

For example, I had gone to see a band perform, out of town, and was enjoying myself at a popular venue. Since I'm a night owl, I would usually stay at a club until closing time, and would then hang out with anyone who wanted to keep the party going, until sunrise.

I walked out at the end of the night with a girl, to make sure she safely got to her car in the dimly-lit parking lot. I was honestly just being a nice, protective guy, because I didn't think anything would develop between us, but I did enjoy our earlier conversation.

After we exited through the backdoor, and walked a few steps, she pushed me back against a wall and planted a passionate kiss on me.

After she pulled back from the kiss, I saw something different in her eyes, so I asked if she would like to stay with me for the night. She agreed to join me, and we ended up in a motel, around 3 AM.

We were in bed, and I kissed her a few times, but there was absolutely no chemistry, whatsoever. I took a little break, made some conversation, then kissed her some more. Again, no sparks. Nothing. She seemed inexperienced and a little nervous, like she wanted to be with me, but was too afraid to actually initiate it.

Even though she seemed open to anything I would want to do, I didn't want to use her for sex, when obviously we weren't clicking. She was giving me a virgin vibe, which I never would have guessed, because she gave the impression that she was tough and streetwise, and that she had been through some rough patches in her life—or maybe it was all just an act.

Underneath the tough-girl exterior, there was something sweet about her. If she was indeed a virgin, I didn't want her first time to be an awkward, nervous encounter in a cheap motel, so I made some small talk and tried to carry a conversation, but we both ended up falling asleep.

The next morning, neither of us said much. We got dressed, wished each other well, said goodbye and went our separate ways.

∽✠∾

A few months later, I was out of town for another show. I was approached by a female who introduced herself and struck up a conversation.

We talked for a while, and she was flirty, so I suggested we leave the club, take a drive and get to know each other better. I said I would later spring for a hotel room, if she wanted, so we could crash, since we had been up all night. She agreed to go, and we hit the highway.

We were on the road for quite a while, and had a lively conversation about music, life, and more, so the vibe was good. We quickly got comfortable with each other, and had a lot of laughs.

After we arrived at a hotel, we walked around the area for a while, then found a secluded spot and made out under the moonlight. We talked and got to know each other much better, and that's when I began hearing things that set off warning bells in my head.

The girl had serious issues, and I wanted no part of that.

In the end, she was fun, but turned out to be a **Tier 3 Crazy** *Party Girl from Hell*, living in a chaotic world, so I didn't even try to get close to her.

We went back to the hotel, and talked a little more, while lying next to each other on the bed. I feigned exhaustion, and eventually went to sleep, because I didn't want to get involved, *at all*.

∾⊷∾

During a period when I was about to end a rotten relationship, and go into one of my Bad Boy phases, I had a close female friend who always supported me, without fail. She had been my friend for a couple of years, was always there for me, made time to hang out, and listened when I felt the need to talk about things.

Our conversations flowed, we laughed, we connected on many levels, we shared secrets, sparks flew between us and she was drama-free. She was also strikingly beautiful, on the inside *and* outside, but I always kept things in check, and on a friendly level.

One day, she mentioned that her computer was malfunctioning, so I offered to go to her place and try to restore it to working condition.

When I arrived, she was very happy to see me, but she seemed nervous. She took me to a spare bedroom where the computer was located, and left me there, while I got to work.

After I diagnosed the problem, and explained what needed to be done to fix it, my friend and I went to the living room and sat. She didn't sit beside me, and she didn't strike up a conversation with me. Instead, she got on the phone with a friend and talked for several minutes. She was fidgeting, acting *very* nervous, and seemed a little breathless at times, but she continued to talk on the phone.

I began to think she was being uncharacteristically rude, ignoring me, while I was a guest in her home. I gave her a few more minutes, but she kept her phone conversation going, so I politely told her that I needed to go.

She finally said goodbye to her friend and ended the call. I put on my leather coat and turned to leave, and she joined me at the door as I was walking out.

She shyly thanked me for working on her computer, and as I turned back to say, "You're welcome," and wish her a good night, she suddenly leaned forward, gave me a fast kiss on the lips, pulled back inside and quickly closed the door.

That's when it hit me: She wasn't being rude; she was trying very hard to be a Good Girl. The phone call (a distraction) and nervousness (attraction, and being alone with me in her home) suddenly made sense.

At that moment, I smiled and felt warmth in my heart for my Good Girl Friend, and thought her gesture was sweet, pure and endearing. I had always found her to be *very* attractive, kind and genuine, but I was technically still in a relationship, even though the woman and I both knew in our hearts that it was over; we just hadn't made any effort to talk and *officially* call it quits.

I thought about it for a moment, and raised my hand to knock on the door. Then it suddenly dawned on me that if she opened that door, all of the Good Guy and Good Girl stuff would quickly be pushed aside, and I would probably end up spending the night with her. That's when I lowered my hand and decided not to knock, because I wasn't a cheater, and I also didn't want my precious Good Girl Friend to compromise her values, or feel overwhelmed. That's the way she felt she needed to handle the situation, so I respected her wishes.

She and I definitely had some things to discuss, about what the future might hold for us, but that wasn't the time to do it—while the sexual tension was very high—so I walked to my car, got in and drove away.

❦

The day that an old girlfriend and I parted ways, I was scheduled to be in Myrtle Beach, South Carolina, to serve as a celebrity judge for the semifinals of a national "battle of the bands" competition. (Several unsigned bands were trying to win cash, equipment and a recording contract.)

The event organizers found me through my writing for an entertainment publication, where I contributed album and concert reviews, band interviews and a music business column.

The girl I was dating was originally planning to go with me, but she was now completely out of the picture, so I decided to make other plans.

At the last minute, I called one of my best female friends. I asked her if she would like to join me for the battle of the bands event, and enjoy an overnight stay at the beach. She agreed, and I picked her up on the way to the coast.

She and I had always been very tight, but we had never dated. She had been to see me perform with an old band, and we regularly called each other on the phone. We talked about anything and everything, loved rock music concerts, and genuinely enjoyed each other's company.

She was very attractive, sweet, high-energy, flirtatious, intelligent and a lot of fun to be around. A man in uniform was more her type of guy, though—and I was the exact *opposite* of all that noise—so I never thought that she and I would ever match up, romantically.

I did not pack any sleepwear, because my ex-girlfriend and I never wore any when we were spending a night together. But since my (now) ex-girlfriend was no longer going to be there, and Girl-Buddy Extraordinaire *was*, I made a point to stop at a store on the way to the beach and pick up something decent to sleep in. I didn't want my friend to be uncomfortable, so I settled on some thin, black sweatpants.

When the event was over, and we got to the hotel room, I saw that my choice of sleepwear didn't really matter, because Girl-Buddy Extraordinaire came to bed in just panties and a t-shirt—a shirt that didn't fully cover her cute, panty-clad behind. I slept in the sweatpants, anyway, just to be a gentleman, but she definitely had my attention!

When I got into bed, I slid over, spooned and hugged her from behind. I thanked her for joining me, and she thanked me for inviting her and returned my hug. We stayed like that for a few seconds, and then I reluctantly broke the hug and went back to my side of the bed. She had a great body, and personality, and I *really* wanted to slide back over to her side of the bed and get something started, but I did nothing.

I felt that she probably would have been open to it, if I had initiated physical contact, but I was still a bit messed up from the break-up.

I had told my friend about my relationship coming to an end, during the drive to the beach, so she probably just left it all in my court, treading lightly through what she perceived to be a delicate situation. It was also possible that she simply felt safe and comfortable around me. But what if she was hoping for something to happen between us, and was disappointed when I didn't make a move to get it started?

In days past, I wondered what would have become of us if I had moved back to her side of the bed. Would she have been receptive? If so, would it have ruined a good friendship, not changed a thing, or would we have dated?

I finally discussed this with her, many years later. She said that she's not exactly sure what would have happened if I had made a move, during that particular time in our lives, but she had always viewed me as more of a "big brother" figure. (The "big brother" thing, again? *Ugh!*)

We didn't click, romantically, and that's okay. It was for the best, since it was probably just my feelings of loneliness and hurt that set the stage for how I was feeling that night—and simply being aroused from having a pretty girl in bed with me—but we're still good friends and still keep in touch.

❧

I know that some men would have handled those situations (above) very differently, but I have learned that I can't change my sense of morality; I'm a Good Guy, with high standards of honor, and that's just how it has to be.

CHAPTER 25

DO NOT INVADE MY GRILLSPACE

For many guys, perfectly cooking cuts of meat on the grill is a badge of honor, a rite of passage, and a gold star on the Masculinity Chart.

Personally, I am not a huge fan of grilling, if I'm the one cooking. I am a creature of efficiency, so taking the time to pour and light charcoal, waiting for it to turn to hot embers, and taking a chance on charring everything is not all that appealing to me, when I could simply whip it up, much faster, in a frying pan on the stove. I'm not really a fan of smoky flavor, either.

When I *do* grill food, though, I don't want anyone interfering with what I'm trying to accomplish!

No, I don't want your advice.

No, I don't need you to remind me how long the food has been cooking on one side.

No, I don't care to hear how you think I'm going to overcook everything.

No, I don't want you to check the temperature.

I don't want you to do a *single thing!*

In all honesty, I prefer my mate to maintain a safe distance of at least 20 feet, and allow me to work my magic without interference. Sorry (not sorry), but that's just how it needs to be in my world.

Wife, if *you* are the Grill Master in your home, your Good Guy husband should show *you* the same courtesies, too. The one who starts the cooking should be left alone, to work their magic in peace—unless the other is *invited* to help, or it is expressly understood that the meal preparation is a joint effort.

I'm just throwing this grilling scenario out there, because you might be surprised at how much resentment and irritation this can cause between you and your man.

CHAPTER 26

THE TOILET SEAT

Seriously, ladies, why is the toilet seat issue such a big deal? The guy lifts it, to make sure you don't get a damp butt when you sit, and he probably leaves it up. You then get bent out of shape. But *why?*

Do you not look down to make sure the seat is in the proper position, before you sit on it, so you don't fall in the bowl? Do your hands not work? Can you not be bothered to set it properly, like everyone else does, before you use it? Your *husband* does. If he didn't, things could get messy for you.

If it really bothers you so much, have a talk with your spouse and work something out—but don't be surprised if you don't get the reaction you want.

In all the years I have been on this earth, I have never heard a man say, "I can't believe she keeps leaving the toilet seat *down!* I always have to lift it!" It's *women* who complain about—and try to control—the toilet seat, not men.

Personally, I always close the lid on the toilet, *completely,* because I just don't like to see the open bowl. I think it looks classier, and can help contain odors, when the lid is closed. Maybe you both could begin to do that, too. That way, both of you will know exactly what to expect, each time you use it.

He will lift it, and so will you. He will close it, and so will you. Sounds like a win-win solution, to me!

Also, toilet paper must *always* roll from over the top of the roll, not from the back and underneath. This is non-negotiable.

CHAPTER 27

THE MAN CAVE

G enerally speaking, and on an instinctual level, men are typically problem solvers. By that, I mean most guys are hardwired to try to fix things (even if we aren't always qualified to do so). We also like to have fun. When we can *combine* the two, it's even better!

I firmly believe in a healthy work-life balance (work hard, play hard), and the Man Cave is where many guys go to unwind, and briefly get some distraction from the real world.

Personally, my Man Cave is my "happy place." It is a room that contains books, framed posters, pictures and other things that remind me of good times. When I walk in, it's instant calm and pleasant memories.

A favorite activity of many men, while in the Man Cave, is playing video games. The games we play give us a lot of opportunities to solve problems and 'fix' a bunch of stuff. Puzzle games, shooting games, racing games and sports titles all tap into our basic problem-solving instincts.

For example, how are we going to get that video game football into the opponent's end zone?

With first-person shooter (FPS) games, *there are people shooting at us!* How do we take them out, first, save ourselves, and one-up those players on the other team?

With role-playing games, how are we going to defeat the dragon and reclaim our treasures, save the princess (why is she always in trouble?), clear out the ghosts and zombies in the haunted mansion, or save the universe from space aliens?

If we pull off a super-human feat in a video game, and are awarded an ultra-rare achievement or trophy, it can be *exhilarating*—and a way for us to brag to our friends— because men are socially competitive; we naturally try to out-do each other, on *everything*, all the time. It's how we bond, and video games provide a perfect opportunity to do that. We get to solve problems and talk trash to other guys when we win!

Some of the happiest couples I know are gamer couples. Even if the wife doesn't actually want to play the games, she will sometimes choose to sit with her husband and watch *him* play the stories, help him solve problems and puzzles, and take pride in her husband's gaming accomplishments—and he loves it.

Men want the fastest car, the most awesome woman, the highest score in a game, etc.—and we want to be able to good-naturedly rub those things in other guys' faces.

Most men need hobbies. Hobbies can also feed the need of problem-solving, while providing a lot of fun—and people usually have more fun with the things they do well.

Take fishing, for another example: How am I going to get a big fish in this boat, and bring home dinner for the family? That task will involve knowing the fish types in the area, and what bait must be used to attract them. Also, you have to know how to use a rod and reel, effectively, or risk losing your catch. Fishing (and hunting) scratches an instinctual hunter-gatherer itch, too.

Again, this is problem-solving, but done in a fun way.

Ladies, I believe that one of the easiest ways to get your Good Guy husband to open up to you is to ask to join him in one of his favorite activities. Good Guys often enjoy talking about, and sharing, their favorite activities and passions.

Try to be respectful and understanding of those things that your man does (within reason) to unwind and have fun. It's just another facet of his personality, and something that can be good for his emotional health.

The Man Cave is a man's sanctuary, and it reflects *his* personality—as opposed to the rest of the house, which probably incorporates more of *your* personality and style (colors, layout, appliances, furniture, pictures, etc.).

Your Good Guy is probably fine with what you want and need in the *rest* of the house, but leave the Man Cave alone.

CHAPTER 28

WHAT A **MAN** WANTS

There is a seemingly endless supply of songs, books, articles, TV dramas, talk shows, podcasts, movies, and more that talk about what a *woman* wants, but what a *man* wants is often overlooked, or completely disregarded—and it's way past time to change that!

Generally speaking—because, again, there are always exceptions to every rule—most Good Guys typically don't need much to be happy. We're actually pretty complex, contrary to what some women seem to think, but we have fairly simple needs and desires.

#1: We want to be appreciated and desired.

Show me a man whose wife regularly shows him that she appreciates him for who he is and what he does, and I'll probably show you a great relationship—and a man who will go to the ends of the earth for his wife. Good Guys love to feel like they are protecting, solving and providing.

The other important things, not in any particular order: Make love to you, and enjoy quality time with you; feel *desired* by you; be true to ourselves; be loved for who we are (without you ladies trying to change us); a little bit of freedom to enjoy hobbies and adventures with friends (always within reason, of course); and have a little "me time" once in a while.

Show me a wife who has her arm around her husband, leaning into him, running her fingers slowly through his hair or rubbing his back, and I'll bet that they are a happy couple.

Most men, in general, like it when their lady initiates physical contact (as long as she isn't constantly *smothering* him with it). A woman doesn't usually touch her man like that if she isn't feeling good about him, so there's something positive there.

Show me a couple where the husband has his arm around his wife, or he is lightly caressing her back or shoulders—and she is obviously enjoying it—and I'll show you another happy couple. A wife who is genuinely receptive to her husband's touch and embrace is a *treasure* to him.

These days, it seems as though it's all about showering the *woman* with attention and gifts, so it is very pleasing to see a woman take her husband's arm, put her arm around him, hold his hand, cuddle up to him, put her head on his chest or shoulder, initiate a kiss, or caress him lovingly.

Personally, I *love* to feel my woman's touch, and I'm not alone in this, when it comes to many other Good Guys.

When my lady casually caresses me, it is extremely soothing and very calming. It is an outward showing of affection that says "I love and appreciate you, and I'm not afraid to show it." Publicly, it also says "This is my man."

Personally, I like that. To me, it's sexy, and an outward showing of our connection. She's kind of marking her territory, just a tiny bit, without being weird or crazy about it. That's fine with me, because I've always been a one-woman kind of guy, anyway, and I do the same thing, sometimes.

Just don't get *possessive*. That's something entirely different—and *crazy*.

There's a difference between being territorial or protective (the desire to protect something you value and cherish), and being jealous (hostile to potential rivals, because of superior qualities, successes, talents or advantages you feel they may possess).

Personally, I can be a little territorial, but I am jealous of no man; I know I have a lot to offer, and I like me the way I am. Are there little things, here and there, that I would improve if I had the chance? Of course. We all feel that way, sometimes, but that doesn't mean that I don't love myself, or that I want to be someone else.

But back to public displays of affection.

Your average Good Guy has probably dealt with some rejection in his life, so for a woman to publicly show that she is happy to be with him, it does a lot for the man.

Since I feel most loved through a woman's physical touch, I love any kind of touching, caressing, kissing, holding her and making love to her. That's how I bond and power-up my emotional batteries. It's like her touch completes an electrical circuit that goes directly to my heart, and I will never get enough of it.

My lady's touch can quickly calm and soothe me, even when I'm at my worst—and I feel that a lot of women do not fully understand just how much *power* they have in their hands (and other wonderful body parts), and what a simple, loving caress can do to calm the "savage beast."

CHAPTER 29

COMPARING HUSBANDS

EMASCULATING YOUR HUSBAND

MEN: COMPETITIVE, WOMEN: COMMUNAL

BUYING A CAR

I'm going to roll all four of those issues into one chapter, since they are closely related.

Ladies, I personally do not know of any Good Guy who appreciates his wife negatively comparing him to another man—especially in front of other people.

Again, each person (yes, even you) has strengths and weaknesses. A smart person is aware of both, and plays to their strengths, while trying to lessen the impact of their weaknesses.

How would you like it if your husband talked about *your* weaknesses and inadequacies in front of other women—or compared you, unfavorably, to a wife of one of his friends? I can read your mind: "He would be sleeping on the couch—or *divorced*—if he did that!" Well, if *you* wouldn't appreciate it, don't do it to your husband, either!

Another reason why men can't stand having their weaknesses shared in public is because men are socially competitive, as I previously mentioned. To emasculate a man is to make him feel less of a man by taking away his masculine power and confidence, and it's even worse when other men are around to witness it.

Women typically like to build community with other women, by connecting, sharing and supporting each other. They often follow the latest fashion trends and lifestyle choices, and like to find common ground.

With many men, *competition* is socializing and bonding—and where all of the "fish tales" and one-upping spring from. Many women don't seem to understand it, or they think it's silly, but that's how we roll. Women can be very competitive, too—and *catty*—but it's a different dynamic.

Calling out a man's flaws and weaknesses undermines his place in the Social Order of Men—and that is *inexcusable*. It's forgivable, but not excusable.

If you take issue with one or more of your husband's flaws or weaknesses, talk with him about it in *private*. Better yet, lovingly help him overcome it! No matter how you work it out, don't emasculate him. Your husband will probably resent you for it, and have a hard time forgiving you.

And don't think that you'll be destroying him in the eyes of his Good Guy friends, if you do it on purpose, out of spite. His friends are most likely going to take him aside, after you've had your little show, and give him support and reassurance—and talk about you like you're some kind of evil creature, sent from Hell, to wreak havoc on earth!

Men are usually competitive, but Good Guys hate to witness a woman beating another good man down, so they will probably rally together *against* you—especially if they've experienced the same thing in their own lives.

～

As for buying a car, I had to throw this one in, just because it personally drives me *insane!*

If I am in the middle of negotiating a deal on a car, please do *not* jump in and offer to help. Almost every time this has happened, it has worked against me when trying to get the deal I wanted—and that means a higher price for the car, and more money out of the budget to pay for it.

If you, wife, are more knowledgeable about cars and making deals, then *you* should be the one negotiating the deal—and your *husband* should butt-out and let you handle it. Either way, the one with the most knowledge and negotiation skills should be the one taking care of business, and the other spouse should chill and let it happen.

That's just one more thing that can cause resentment in a relationship—especially if you get stuck with many years of paying a higher monthly payment than you wanted.

CHAPTER 30

WHY ARE YOU TALKING TO MY EX?

I have never understood the thing about a wife or girlfriend bumping into their man's ex-girlfriend or ex-wife, in public, and then ending up in a conversation about the man, after they have been introduced. Yes, it seems to be rare, but it does happen.

The women eventually begin comparing notes, discussing what the previous relationship was like, the little annoying (or cute) things they've noticed about him, etc., and actually *bond* over it! I understand that women are generally communal, but that's just too much.

The woman is an ex for a reason, so I don't want *any* influence or interference whatsoever from her in our current relationship.

Good Guys usually don't do weird stuff like that. Typically, we want *nothing* to do with your ex. If he's around, and you don't tell us, and you let us meet and hang out, that is often a deal-breaker. We usually don't want to be around anyone that you have been intimate with in the past—especially if *they* know it, and we don't.

Since men are generally competitive and hierarchical, Bad Boys love to let it be known that they've slept with the new guy's woman. A Good Guy usually doesn't even want to *think* about the woman he loves being intimate with another man, and that's why the Bad Boys do it: to hurt him and attempt to show dominance.

Sometimes, the Bad Boy will try to keep everything quiet, hoping to get close to the woman again, without the new guy knowing any better. That's why a guy might feel like there's something up, when his girl never mentions that an ex-boyfriend is still hanging around—and her loyalty will be determined by which man she decides to protect.

On a purely *primal, biological and instinctual level*, if a woman has sex with a guy, it seems to me that she basically finds him to be qualified, in some way, to be a potential father of children (not necessarily a dad, or husband, though). That is why some men can be protective: Women always know that they are the mothers of their naturally-conceived children, but men can never be *one-hundred percent sure* that they are the fathers—and why they try to prevent the possibility that another man might try to sneak one in.

In my opinion, one of the most evil things a woman can ever do is let her man believe that another man's child is his, with all of the emotional and financial investment that will be made in raising it—and the devastation that could utterly *destroy* many lives and relationships, including the life of the child, if the truth is discovered.

CHAPTER 31

CONFIDENCE IS SEXY

Many women are not pleased with themselves, physically—and they *constantly* let us know it (*ugh!*). They complain about all kinds of things that are "wrong" with their bodies, and are never satisfied—and I know a lot of husbands who are so very tired of hearing it!

Your Good Guy married *you*, for many reasons. He probably doesn't appreciate you constantly putting down the woman he loves.

So, you have a couple of things you would change about yourself, if you could. Guess what? We *all* do! Big deal! No one is perfect. Even many supermodels you see in magazines have issues—and their photos and layouts are digitally altered and enhanced to hide their imperfections.

Your Good Guy wants you to love yourself as much as *he* loves you. He wants you to be happy and confident.

Having a *healthy* awareness of your body can be a positive thing for your well-being and improving your overall health, but don't let those things interfere with you enjoying your husband, and your husband enjoying you, in bed.

"Beautiful" is a *very* subjective term; each person has his or her own idea of what is beautiful, with just about anything you can imagine—flowers, babies, art, cars, dresses, the color of someone's eyes, jewelry, shoes, hairstyles, houses, wedding dresses, you name it. We all have our personal preferences, and they can vary, wildly, from one person to the next.

Some people like blondes, and some people like brunettes—or redheads. Some folks prefer a petite body type, while others prefer their mate to be more full-figured. Some people like long hair, and some people like shorter styles. Some folks love the color blue, while others prefer yellow. The point is that there is no official standard for what is beautiful, and what is not; it all depends on the viewer.

If your husband tells you how hot you are, how he loves touching you, he wants to kiss you all over, or what you are doing feels incredible, while you're in bed together, *believe it!* Remember that many men feel loved through a physical connection, so he is genuinely having an unforgettable, fulfilling, loving, emotional experience with you, and *telling* you so. He is exactly where he wants to be: intimately connected with *you.*

Don't let the world tell you that you aren't beautiful, or you don't measure up. Know your worth, and listen to the Good Guy who loves you, who married you, who wants to look at you, hold you, make love to you, have children with you and create a wonderful family with you! *His* words should far outweigh *anything* the rest of the world has to say!

Preferences and turn-ons are different for each person, so believe it when your husband says that he thinks you're smokin' hot—and don't hide when you catch him looking at you. Enjoy his attention and affection, and be *empowered* by it!

In addition, if there's something sexual you want to do, have the confidence to tell him! All of the Good Guys I know would be absolutely *thrilled* to hear their wives boldly suggest something new to try. Again, since many Good Guys have experienced rejection in their lives, having their lovely wives initiate a sexual connection is absolutely *amazing!*

The overwhelming majority of men, across the board, are highly turned on by seeing, feeling and hearing their wife experiencing sexual pleasure from what they are doing to her, so if there's something you want to try that you think will bring you pleasure, I feel very confident that your Good Guy husband would jump at the chance to try it.

If you are losing control, breathing heavily, making noises, and squirming around on the bed, because of how your Good Guy is pleasuring you, it's one of the most beautiful things in the world to him. It's also instinctual and logical: If you have a great experience, you're more likely to come back for more—and, on a *primal* level, that gives us another opportunity to pass on our genetic information.

Your body language and verbal feedback also let us know when we're getting it right, and giving you what you need, so let yourself go! Don't hesitate to let us see, hear and feel it, so we can learn what you like.

Your pleasure is the key to making it great. When you are feeling good, and really into it, your Good Guy works harder to please you—and he has orgasms that are much more intense, so it's an incentive for him, too.

CHAPTER 32

HIS SILENCE

M en and women are very different animals. Women seem more prone to lay it all on the table, or wear their emotions on their sleeves, but men tend to say something serious when they have something serious to say.

If your Good Guy husband doesn't have anything to add, or needs time to think about the things you've said— or if he thinks that *anything* he says will only make things worse—he might remain silent. It doesn't mean he's scared, doesn't care, or isn't supportive; it just means that he doesn't have a *solution*, or doesn't want to aggravate the situation.

Remember, we try to *solve* problems, so we look for solutions. A solution isn't usually what you want, so that's where the anger and resentment can creep in, because of the different ways men and women approach a problem.

Give your man time to digest what you've said. Once he has something to add, he should let you know.

If he gets sidetracked by life—or is a little hesitant to respond, for previously-mentioned reasons—*gently* remind him of your conversation in a day or two. Let him know that you truly value his input, and how he feels. *Calmly and respectfully*, ask if he has anything to add. (Guys, you should have a solid answer for her, by then.)

On a side note, let's say we're just chatting, and we say something that gives you pause. Out of all the ideas and possible explanations that immediately pop into your head, we did not mean *any* of the bad ones. Honestly, we did not, so please don't misunderstand, or immediately jump to negative conclusions.

CHAPTER 33

TUNING OUT

It's true; men can blank-out and not think about anything, at all. And if a man *is* thinking about something, while he's staring off into space, it's often something benign, such as work; he wants to join his beautiful wife in the shower; it's been a while since he's had a good hotdog; he wants to drop certain candies into a bottle of cola, and watch it erupt like a volcano; his car needs new tires; dinosaurs were cool, etc.

If your man blanks-out, don't sweat it; he'll zap back to reality in a bit. He isn't ignoring you; his mind is just wandering around. It's natural.

Men also have a unique special ability, when it comes to tuning out, but you aren't going to like it: We can tune out repeated sounds or unwanted noise. That includes *you*, sometimes, too—especially when you're nagging, or going on and on about something completely uninteresting to us.

I've read that this gift to men—yes, *gift*—is due to testosterone playing a part in our auditory development, before we were born. Apparently, gracious God knew we would need breaks, so he included that ability in our development, while we were still in the womb! (Hallelujah!)

All joking aside, sometimes our blank-out just happens without us even realizing it. That's when you say, "Are you even listening to me?" and we suddenly snap back to reality, realizing what has happened, trying not to seem insensitive.

A Good Guy will work hard (but not always succeed) to keep this ability in check, to make sure he is paying attention to his wife and giving her the kind of emotional connection that she wants and needs.

CHAPTER 34

BELIEVE IT OR NOT

Sometimes, your Good Guy husband might actually turn down an opportunity to make love to you (*gasp!*). Don't act so shocked, or stereotype men as being all-consumed with sex.

Yes, most men I've encountered want a steady, healthy sex life, but the outside world can affect a man just as it can a woman—and I'm speaking from personal experience.

If your marriage is healthy, and your husband turns down an opportunity to make love with you, saying he's too tired or stressed to adequately perform, it's a very good bet he's genuinely tired and doesn't want to disappoint you—or *himself*, because performance can be very important to a man.

If turning down lovemaking is becoming a regular occurrence, though, and causing problems in your marriage, you may want to see a doctor or counselor. High stress and exhaustion aren't healthy for anyone.

There could be other physical, hormonal, age-related or emotional issues involved, also, and certain medications can affect a person's sex drive, as well. The same goes for women, too.

Having *mismatched* sex drives can also cause serious problems in marriage. If that's the case, respectful, open and honest communication is vital to reaching a compromise that both of you can accept.

If there are physical issues, with either of you, that make it difficult or even impossible to have vaginal intercourse, there are many other ways of sexually satisfying each other. Get creative, and explore the many different ways that you can still enjoy sexual intimacy and pleasure.

If physical conditions or mental barriers are keeping *either* of you from fully enjoying lovemaking, contact a licensed healthcare provider in your area for an assessment and possible treatment options.

CHAPTER 35

VIOLENCE IS <u>ALWAYS</u> UNACCEPTABLE

Period. End of story. Initiating violence against someone can be physically and emotionally damaging.

Personally, I don't even like to be slapped on the arm when someone is trying to get my attention, or they're surprised by something I've added to a conversation. It instantly activates my robotic "AIRSPACE VIOLATION! ELIMINATE TARGET!" response.

You've probably seen it, the "Shut! Up! That is *crazy!*" reaction, along with the back-handed arm slap. It's very irritating. It's a violation of my person, and my personal airspace bubble. You don't have to do that to get my attention. (If you do, I probably didn't want to talk to you, in the first place.)

In movies and TV shows, there are many scenes of women slapping or punching men, and that seems to be okay, as if the men deserve it and should just stand there and take it. The women, though, get a pass, or are celebrated.

I have read and heard stories and songs about women using baseball bats to destroy their cheating men's cars, for example. Sadly, it seems to me that this has turned into some type of "women empowerment," and a "You go, girl! Serves him right!" kind of thing.

If the roles were reversed, and a man on the evening news was shown destroying his cheating *girlfriend's* car, I have no doubt that there would be many women, and women's organizations, protesting violence against women, and shouting how the man's actions "send the wrong message" about how to deal with anger and relationship issues.

I would agree with their cries for people to engage in peaceful conflict resolution, but I would also expect those same women to protest, just as loudly, when a *woman* was violent, too.

The point is that the double standard for violent behavior has to end! If violence is bad for one, it's bad for *all*.

It doesn't matter if your husband can take it, because maybe he's a big man and you're a smaller woman. If your husband hit *you*, it would be considered Criminal Domestic Violence (CDV), regardless of his size or reason, and another "violence against women" situation. It's unacceptable for your husband to hit you, and it's also unacceptable for you to hit your husband. Even if your husband can take it, all day long, it's still violent and hurtful—and should never happen.

It's not about hardiness or manliness; it's about the fact that you're *hitting* someone. It's total disrespect. The violence can leave physical and emotional scars, create rifts and cause resentment that may be nearly impossible to heal.

If you introduce violence into your marriage, your husband might get the idea that if violence is good for you, it's good for *him*, too—or, being a Good Guy, he holds it all in, which can also be very bad, because you never know if someone will eventually snap and explode.

If you feel that things are getting overheated, and you are on the verge of losing your temper, respectfully state that you need to step away and take time to cool down. Revisit the issue at a later time, when you can talk in a mature and respectful manner, you are calm, and you are fully in control of your emotions.

If you need assistance with controlling your anger, reach out to a healthcare or mental health professional, and ask for help with anger management.

Violence is always a *very* bad idea for your relationship, and each other's health!

CHAPTER 36

DON'T READ <u>ANYTHING</u> INTO WHAT WE SAY

You: "Do these pants look good on me? Be honest."
Him: "Not really."
You: (feel like your butt is too big and get self-conscious and upset.)
Him: "What is it? You told me to be honest!"

Men often look at things very differently from the ways women view things.

You asked if the *pants* looked good *on* you, not if *you* looked good in the pants. In his way of thinking, *you*, his beautiful wife, *always* look good, but some pants just fit better, and are more appealing than others. It's the *pants*, not you.

If you feel insulted or hurt by an answer (something we Good Guys would never *intentionally* do), please politely ask us to explain. Don't automatically assume the worst.

If you don't want to take the chance of receiving an answer you won't like, you're the type who immediately jumps to the worst conclusions, or you're easily offended, you might want to reconsider asking the question, in the first place.

CHAPTER 37

SPEED DEMONS & BACKSEAT DRIVERS

One of my earliest memories is of me sitting on my maternal grandfather's lap, and him letting me take the wheel of his light-blue Volkswagen Beetle. We were cruising down one of the city's main streets, headed away from town, and I still remember the exact spot when I took over. I couldn't reach the pedals, but I was keeping us on the road and in our lane!

My grandfather was a great, wise man, but he didn't like to wait around on a "slowpoke," in traffic—and neither do I. When he was driving, he wanted everyone to pull over to the side of the road and let him pass, unhindered—and so do I.

If he got behind a slowpoke, he would get impatient and start shouting, "C'mon, c'mon!" as if it would make any difference. (Speaking from experience, it doesn't.)

I often enjoy taking a drive, since it's also when I most often listen to my heavy music, or talk radio shows—and I don't like to creep along, while I'm doing it. The need for speed is definitely part of my DNA, from my grandfather.

Ladies, let's get a few things straight, when it comes to guys like me:

Don't tell us how to drive—especially when you do a lot of the same things you complain about (speed, tailgate, impatiently pass a car) when *you* drive! And constant criticism distracts us, when we should be focusing on the road.

If your husband is behind a slowpoke, and he floors it to get past, and the other guy speeds up to prevent him from passing, and it turns into a race, please don't freak out. It's what a lot of guys do.

Remember the whole "one-up" thing? The struggle is real, no matter how silly it may seem to you.

CHAPTER 38

YOUR FINGERNAILS

If your fingernails are so long that they render your fingers useless for doing everyday tasks, we (men) can't take you seriously. Rendering your fingers useless, in order to make a fashion statement, makes you look ridiculous when trying to figure out how to do things.

For example, I can't tell you how many times I've been in a checkout line at a retail store and witnessed a woman experiencing difficulties, because of mile-long nails. I can't help it; I almost laugh out loud, as I watch her twist, turn and stretch her fingers in an effort to tap a selection on a credit card terminal, or retrieve coins from her purse— and then I get irritated, because her vanity is holding up the line!

Elegant, natural nails are nice, but ridiculously-long, useless "vanity claws" are not.

And just so you know, all of the vanity stuff that a man sees on you gives him an indication of the lifestyle you want to lead, and how *expensive* life might become, in a relationship with you.

CHAPTER 39

IT'S NOT A COMPETITION

If your Good Guy has been next to you at the dinner table, or on the couch, and you've had absolutely nothing to say to him for a very long time, don't interrupt and try to get him to talk to you once he decides to go off and do something else on his own—like turning on the TV and getting involved in a football game, for example. If you do, it looks like you're purposely being controlling and needy—or you're trying to punish him, by interrupting his good time, for something that you've kept bottled up inside.

Your husband would probably be thrilled to have you join and watch the game with him, but please don't suddenly remember that there is something important you wanted to talk to him about, or something you wanted him to do, as soon as he goes off on his own. If you do, you're probably going to lose that battle. He can talk to you at any time after it's over, but he only has a chance to watch a *live* game as it's happening—and you've waited this long, so what's the sudden rush?.

Being able to "talk sports" with the guys, the next day, is also part of male bonding and competition for some guys, so it can be very important to him to be up to speed on the day's sporting events.

Remember these things: 1) You are not in a competition with whatever it is he's doing; 2) whatever he's doing truly isn't as important as you; 3) he shouldn't have to stop, just to prove it to you and soothe your insecurities, every time; and 4) by waiting around, for hours, and pouncing on him only after he has walked away and gotten involved with something else, you're being controlling.

If you try to force him to choose, you may just lose the fight, because some Good Guys are rebellious (like me), and we may rebel even if it makes things worse, simply because we refuse to be controlled.

There is a time and place for everything. If needing to talk to him about something was really *that* important, you wouldn't have waited so long before speaking up.

CHAPTER 40

DRAMA QUEENS

When you get angry, whine and want to argue over silly and insignificant things, even though your man is a Good Guy he still thinks you're being a petty, needy and ridiculous drama queen—and he secretly questions your level of maturity.

Take a moment and ask yourself, "Is this little thing really so important and life-altering, in the grand scheme of things, that I'm willing to take a chance on ruining my relationship over it?" If the answer is "no," think twice about making a fuss.

Part of being in a relationship is learning to tolerate your partner's minor quirks, style differences and idiosyncrasies. Yes, they can be annoying at times, but if they aren't deal breakers, and they can be avoided, try to be understanding and let things slide. If you can't get past them, try to be thoughtful and kind if you address them with your spouse.

Whatever you do, kindly and calmly *ask*—not whine or demand—him to consider how you feel, when it comes to those issues. And if things don't work out exactly as you hoped, try not to let them ruin your relationship, if things are good, otherwise.

If you see that something small is turning into a big issue in your relationship, take time to thoughtfully, calmly and respectfully work it out, as soon as possible, before it gets a chance to grow into something you can't overcome.

Your Good Guy is probably also dealing with *your* irritating quirks and mannerisms, too, so he should receive equal consideration.

CHAPTER 41

NEW DAY, NEW WAY

Your eyes and touch have tremendous power over your husband. When you get very close, put your arms around his neck, and look into his eyes with that soft-but-very-serious, "I *love* this man" feminine look of longing, you probably have the ability to ignite a *fire* within him, pretty easily.

There are very few things that go right to the core of a man's soul like a woman who has that soft but intense look of true love, appreciation and *desire* in her eyes. Your face tells the story, without having to say a word, and your Good Guy husband probably loves and *craves* it.

When you don't hold back, and you make your desire for him clear, he gets lost in you. He wants to pleasure you, feel you, and connect with you.

Tonight, take your time making love. Include lots of touching, caressing, and kissing. Laugh a little, and have some fun. Add in some light conversation about what you love about each other, how you're enjoying the things you're doing to each other (men *love* positive feedback in the moment), and how much you truly love one another.

The next day—especially if the two of you haven't been sexually intimate, lately—your husband might say something like, "Last night was *amazing!* What made you decide that you wanted us to be together? Not that I'm complaining, or anything, *believe* me, because I thoroughly enjoyed it. You were *incredible!*"

You could cozy up to him and reply with something like, "Well, we haven't been together in a while, and I wanted us to be close again and reconnect—and I really enjoyed it, too, as you could easily tell.

"Maybe this could be a fresh start. Let's make a conscious effort to stay connected, support one another, talk more, have fun, share what's going on in our lives, and spend more quality time with each other.

"I know that you feel the most loved and connected to me when we touch, so I wanted to remind you of how much I love and appreciate you—and I promise to show you, more often. I want *you* to show *me* those kinds of things, too.

"I want us to be great together."

With that, you just burst through the doors of your Good Guy's castle (heart), conquered it, and planted your banner atop the highest tower! He feels more emotionally connected to you, and *talkative*, so it has just become easier for you to reach your husband and connect with him on the type of emotional level that *you* desire.

Husband, return the favor and give your wife the things that make *her* feel connected and loved, too. She can't be the only one making an effort, or it won't last.

CHAPTER 42

"WHERE DO YOU WANT TO EAT?"

Him: "Whatever you want is fine with me."

Her: "I want you to pick a place that you like."

Him: "It's fine, really. Just pick a restaurant. I'm sure I can find something on the menu, wherever we go. If I was truly in the mood for something very specific—which is rare—I would tell you."

Her: "I wish you would just pick something."

Him: "I *always* have to pick. Why can't you just decide on something and be done with it? When I tell you that I'm fine with whatever you choose, I really am fine with whatever you choose. It's not rocket science; it's just lunch."

Her: (Gets irritated and quiet.)

Him: (Not understanding how something so simple could be so complicated, he activates the car's turn signal in frustration.) "Fine. I'm just going to pull in here, then."

Her: "I don't like that place."

Him: (He is now about to lose his mind!)

Ladies, if we say that we don't care where we go to eat, we really don't care where we go to eat! Please, just choose something that will make you happy, and we'll go with it.

If we truly do not care for a particular place, we will let you know. And if we do happen to mention that a certain restaurant isn't to our liking, or we just aren't in the mood for that type of food, don't shut down on us and give up. It's not a rejection of *you*; it's the restaurant.

The choice of where to go for a meal is often and happily given to the wife, out of respect. We figure if we give the her the choice, she will be happy with her decision and enjoy the meal—and we *definitely* want her to be happy.

If she enjoys the meal, she will be in a better mood. If she is in a better mood, we will get along better. If we are getting along better, we can have positive interactions. If we have positive interactions, we will be much more emotionally-connected. If we are more emotionally connected, *we might make love, tonight!*

I told you that men are more complex than you might think.

CHAPTER 43

"IT'S NOTHING."

Those words mean very different things to men and women.

Him: "It's something I can fix. No big deal."
Her: "There's a problem, and you should know what it is without me having to tell you!"

Do yourself a favor: Skip the drama and tell him what's bothering you. By doing so, you will save yourself a lot of time and irritation.
We aren't mind readers, remember?

CHAPTER 44

DON'T TALK DOWN TO ME

You wanted an argument? Well, congratulations! You just started one.

Being condescending is never going to win you any favors, debates or arguments. The only thing it's going to do is make someone feel hurt, angry, dismissive or resentful—or you may get a smart aleck, like me, that attempts to show you just how ridiculous you are for even *trying* that silly stunt.

Please, don't do that to *anyone*.

You want others to treat *you* with respect, so show others the respect you want to receive.

CHAPTER 45

CHARITY

The Bible tells us to be charitable, and not to close our hands to the poor. It also says that if we boast about what we do for someone else, it is as if we didn't do anything at all, in God's eyes.

The Bible also tells us that forcing someone to be charitable isn't charity, at all, because God views charity as something being done with a willing, uncoerced and cheerful heart.

Taxation, even for what is presented as a "good cause," cannot be considered charity, either, because forced extraction of wealth is a morally unacceptable way to provide funding.

If someone is forced, gives out of some sense of obligation, or does it begrudgingly, it isn't charity; the person is doing it simply because he feels he's supposed to, has no choice, or he's trying to avoid perceived negative consequences from not doing it (public scorn, family shame, being ridiculed or shunned, etc.). If it isn't done out of love, it isn't charity, plain and simple.

When someone attempts to do something nice for me, my first instinct is to reject it; I like to think of myself as being independent and capable of taking care of my needs. I don't want someone else's help, money, or anything else. I appreciate the thought, but I'd rather take care of things on my own—and that's a behavior that God had to break in me.

God wants us to be charitable, so when someone attempts to bless us with a thoughtful act of kindness, we should graciously accept it and be thankful that God used that person to bless us. We should not try to stop the person from doing what God has asked of us all, because not only would we miss out on the blessing that the other person has to give, we would also stop the other person from receiving a blessing from doing the kinds of things that God wants us to do for each other. Surely, a person is blessed for even having made an attempt to do something kind for someone else, but knowing that a charitable act is appreciated and thankfully accepted is a blessing to the giver, also.

Charity isn't just about giving money to a worthy cause; you can be charitable with your time, talents, skills, knowledge, wisdom, or just offering a helping hand to someone.

For example, you can bake a cake for a friend, help with house cleaning, pick up trash beside the road, cheer up your spouse with a surprise evening out on the town, draw a special picture for someone, pay for the meal of the person behind you in the drive-up line, help a friend change a flat tire, buy a break-time snack for a coworker, take a grocery order to someone who has mobility issues, treat a friend to lunch, etc.

Bad things sometimes happen to good people, and life has a way of throwing curveballs our way. Acts of charity and kindness can help to keep relationships solid and durable, and lift people out of despair when they feel alone, desperate or hopeless.

Any act of kindness, or gift—that is freely given, and done out of love—is charity, and God blesses those who are charitable.

Acts of love and charity are important to any type of relationship, so be willing to help others, and allow others to help you.

CHAPTER 46

INFIDELITY

In studying relationships and marriages, I have noticed a big uptick in the number of articles, TV shows, magazines, movies and books that promote infidelity (adultery) as a way to "spice things up," "have it all!" or "relieve some stress" in your marriage—especially if you're a lonely housewife who feels unappreciated and overworked. "You deserve to feel loved, appreciated and *desired*," they preach. And if your husband isn't giving you what you want, what better way to get it than to have a secret affair, right?

Wrong!

One of the worst things you can ever do to yourself or your spouse is "cheat" with someone else. Cheating involves sexual intimacy with someone other than your spouse.

Some people never get over the devastation that cheating can cause, and it can easily and forever extinguish the positive light in someone. I have seen it happen, too many times—and I, too, have never been the same since I was first cheated on, when I was a young man.

Generally speaking, Good Guys are the gentlemanly types who have had their share of heartbreak and rejection, so when they find someone with whom they truly bond and commit, they can grow roots that run pretty deep in the relationship—which means that they can suffer even greater damage, because of the deeper attachment and lack of a large support system from other men (being competitive, not communal).

Cheating hits people right in the heart, and scores a direct, devastating hit on some of our greatest fears and insecurities. Too often, it can cause withdrawal, feelings of despair, low self-esteem, obsessive behaviors, denial, lasting distrust, easily-triggered defense mechanisms, a loss of direction in life, chronic anxiety, self-loathing, hatred, even suicide. It can easily push a person into a very dark place.

"What did I do wrong?"

"Am I not pretty enough?"

"Am I not manly enough?"

"I don't want to live in this world, anymore. My life is over."

"Am I a bad person?"

"This proves that no one will ever truly love me."

"I'm a failure."

"God has forsaken me."

If you ever get to a point where you feel unappreciated, are bored with your everyday routine, don't feel connected to your spouse the way you used to, feel like you've become roommates instead of husband and wife, feel like you or your husband has "checked out," etc., I beg you to take a moment and think about what you really want in your relationship. Set a date and time to sit down and thoughtfully, calmly, lovingly and *respectfully* share those feelings and desires with your spouse, instead of *ever* entertaining the idea of being with someone else. Never break the marriage vows that you made.

You fell in love, and got married, because of the wonderful feelings you had for your spouse. It may not be easy, but put your egos aside, work to bring those feelings back and renew your love for each other.

CHAPTER 47

THE POWER OF WORDS

In the Bible, Proverbs 18:21 says that life and death are in the power of the tongue, and you will eat the fruit thereof, depending upon the types of things you say to others.

Ephesians 4:29 says to not let any kind of corrupt communication come from your mouth, but say good and positive things that build others up.

Your words have the power to tear someone down, and leave them devastated and suicidal, just as easily as they can lift someone out of darkness, give them hope, and let them know that they have a friend who will be there to support them.

Also, anger can be a powerful motivator, but it has to be controlled and contained, or it can consume and destroy everything it touches. You must take good care to ensure that the things you say, while angry, do not destroy others. You can still be angry, and calmly confront someone who has wronged you, but using hateful, destructive, vulgar words, to try to hurt or enrage goes against Biblical teaching.

Let your anger motivate you to work out a correction to an offensive, dangerous or hurtful situation, but always choose your words and tone carefully and wisely, because nasty insults and provocation usually get in the way of resolution, forgiveness and reconciliation.

Additionally, Proverbs 18:13 says that having an answer for a situation, before finding out what's truly happening, is folly and shameful, so *listen* and get the facts, before choosing a course of action.

CHAPTER 48

VALENTINE'S DAY

One of the historical accounts I've read about the possible origins of Valentine's Day reportedly involved a Catholic priest from Rome, named Valentine de Terni, who was blessed with great gifts of healing.

According to the legend, Emperor Claudius II issued an unpopular edict that forbade marriages and engagements, because he felt that marriage would keep men from joining the army, distract the soldiers, and decrease effectiveness and efficiency in battle. Valentine was beheaded for performing secret weddings, and spreading Christianity, in spite of the emperor's orders condemning those practices.

The legend also states that Valentine healed the jailer's blind daughter, Julia, and then converted the jailer's entire family to Christianity, after the miracle was performed.

On the day of his execution, Valentine is said to have left a note for Julia, signed "Your Valentine," which supposedly gave rise to celebrating his martyrdom. In modern times, it has evolved into exchanging cards and notes of love and friendship—valentines—on the anniversary of his execution, February 14th.

According to the legend, many soldiers, and the women who loved them, chose to defy the government—and risk death—to be married.

Throughout history, it seems that governments have had a bad habit of interfering in personal relationships, and I feel that no one should have to get permission (a license) from government, or pay fees (bribes), in order to be "allowed" (a word that would never be used in a truly free society) to marry—but that's another story, for another day.

I'm going to switch gears and clue you in on something that's very important: Valentine's Day isn't just for women! It's a day to celebrate love and marriage. It isn't just to make the *woman* feel special; the *man* should be made to feel special, too!

Go back to how you and your spouse each feel most loved and appreciated, and plan things that best send those messages of love to each other.

Does your spouse love to hear your words of encouragement and affirmation? A great Valentine's Day gift might be, among other special tokens of love and affection, a card with a special handwritten note that says all of those supportive and encouraging things.

Does your spouse feel most loved during times of physical and sexual intimacy with you? I'm sure the gift that fits into *this* scenario is quite obvious.

If your spouse feels most loved when you do things around the house, surprise him or her with a completed repair, a clean and organized home, their favorite meal, or some other work that saves your spouse time and effort.

Whatever you do for each other, take time to enjoy spending quality time together. Reconnect, romance each other and add a good bit of fun. Make it a day to remember!

Most women I've spoken with say that connection, romance and fun shouldn't be reserved for just one special day a year, though; they want those things kept alive and well, all year long.

CHAPTER 49

THE POWER OF A WOMAN'S GENTLE SPIRIT

To paraphrase 1 Peter 3:1 in the Holy Bible, even if your husband isn't following the Word of God, you can be a Christian example to him, with a gentle and loving spirit, and possibly win him over without even having to say a word! According to the Bible, you have a *lot* of power and influence in your marriage (or committed relationship, if you haven't tied the knot, yet), if you will decide to use it.

If any Good Guy husbands are reading this, 1 Peter also states that you are to honor your wives, and dwell with them with *understanding*, so that your prayers will be unhindered.

And just so we're *very* clear, guys, a wife's biblical submission to you does *not* mean that she's supposed to be your servant, beneath you, or obey your commands. Marriages where husband and wife have an equal voice, have equal power in decision-making, and work together as a team, have a *much* better chance of standing the test of time.

You, husband, are called to be the spiritual leader in your household, being a Christian example for your wife and children. You are charged with creating an atmosphere where your wife feels confident, safe and happy in following, supporting and submitting to your Christian leadership in the home.

The saying goes, "Behind every good man is a good woman." I'm not convinced of that, actually, since I've met a lot of good men who never had the support of a good woman, but I can tell you that it definitely makes things a lot better—and *easier*—when you do!

I speak from experience, when the Bible says that a woman can lead her man to God through her example. Actually, in my case, it was *back* to God.

I had always believed in God, and had accepted Jesus when I was young, but I had strayed from living the Christian life for many years. That all changed, later in adulthood.

The woman I was with, at the time, went to church on Sunday mornings. I would always decline to go with her, because I didn't care to be around people who I thought were "playing church" on Sundays. I knew that I was a sinner, and had fallen short of the glory of God, so I wasn't going to act all saved and sanctified just on Sunday. I wasn't living my life the way God intended, but I wasn't going to lie about it, either, the way I thought many Christians were doing.

Each week, my lady would go to church, and I could tell that she was disappointed, heartbroken, and lonely in going alone. She would often extend a very gentle invitation to join her, but she wouldn't press the point if I declined to go—and *that* made all the difference in the world.

She would sometimes let me know that she would love for me to join her, but by not being pushy, shaming, holier-than-thou, pouty, whiny or arguing with me about it, it didn't push me away from the idea.

Actually, thinking back on it, it seems that my Knight in Shining Armor side kind of kicked in and got me thinking about joining her, if for no other reason than to make her happier.

If I went with her to church, I would be doing it for *her*, not the church people—at least, that's how I justified it in my brain. But no matter the line of reasoning that got me back into it all, the point is that I starting going to church again, and it was all because of her example. She was living the behavior that she wanted to see in *me*.

After she broke through to me on going to church, and I got used to regularly attending, God decided to take things a step further.

I began seeing street signs for one particular Christian contemporary church, all over town. I even came into contact with—and got a personal invitation from—a married couple that volunteered at that church, through a coworker at a former job.

I had never attended a Christian contemporary service, and wasn't sure I would like it, but something in my head kept telling me to give the church a try, because I was looking for something new. I spoke to my sweetie, and she was fine with it. Actually, I think she was fine with going to just about *any* church, as long as it meant I continued to attend each week.

We decided to check out the new church, which was about a half-hour away. We were greeted by many people, and made to feel very welcome, as soon as we walked through the door.

During the service, I remember thinking that the music and production were low-budget, but it seemed like the musicians' hearts were in the right place. I also made a point to shake the young pastor's hand, and tell him that I enjoyed the service, as we seemed to be fairly similar in our ways of looking at the world, based upon his sermon that day.

After the service was over, my partner and I were given some gifts for being first-time guests, then we exited the building and got into my car.

Before I even turned the key, I looked over to her and asked, "So, what did you think?" She was very pleased, and I felt the same way, so we decided to start going to the new church.

Church volunteers discovered that I was a drummer, so they began encouraging me to play drums with them, but there was no way I was getting involved in church activities, again. I just wanted to sit on the sidelines, not be bothered, and go in peace, but God had very different plans for me.

We started attending the contemporary church in early June of that year. In November, the church opened a new campus in my town—conveniently located, about three minutes from my house—and they needed musicians.

What a coincidence, right? No, not at all. I firmly believe that it was part of God's plan for me.

Long story short, I ended up being the main drummer at the new church campus, which eventually became the main campus. I played the drums for nearly every service, for the three years that I volunteered to be a part of the worship team. In doing so, I began to open up, soften up, see certain things in a new light, and grow as a Christian.

Now, I'm a better man, trying to walk the righteous path, and I have started ministry work of my own.

I believe that God crosses our paths with certain people and places for a reason, and each new season of life brings about change and opportunities for growth.

I wish nothing but the very best for each person who was there, during that particular season, and I am very thankful that the woman who was in my life, at that time, provided the kind of example I needed to get back on the right path.

CHAPTER 50

FROM WHOM ALL BLESSINGS FLOW

B lessings come in many forms, and God even says in
Malachi 3:10 that we can challenge Him on His
promise to bless us when it comes to tithing (giving 10%
of our earnings to God).

Some pastors preach a "prosperity doctrine" (if you
tithe, you will be rewarded with money and wealth) based
on this verse, but nowhere does it say that you will get
financially rich due to tithing. Though some blessings can
indeed come in the form of money and physical wealth,
the Bible simply says you will be *blessed*—and blessings
come in many forms.

Let me give you just a few of the many examples of
how I, personally, have been blessed over the years,
ranging from very small matters to life-changing events.

⋘

There have been a couple times when I wasn't sure
how I was going to make it through to the end of the week,
needing gas in the car, because I was financially "broke." I
had prayed for help, and just when it seemed all was lost, I
found a few bills in a pants pocket. I usually don't carry
cash, so *I* didn't put it there, and I didn't ask anyone for a
small loan. I asked God, and I received just what I needed.

⋘

When I was a young boy, a lady in our church asked
for prayer. She had late-stage cancer, but believed that
God would intervene and heal her.

All of the people who were in attendance went down
to the altar with her. She knelt, the pastor anointed her
head with oil, and we laid our hands upon her, as the

Bible instructs. We prayed for her healing, believing that God would deliver a miracle.

When our church friend went for her next appointment, her doctor found *no trace* of cancer in her body, and that blessing—which science cannot explain—has stayed with me, my entire life. My belief in God, and His miraculous power, has never left me, and I'm very thankful that I was able to witness, and be a part of, that life-changing experience.

Remembering that miracle—and many others that I have witnessed over the years—has often kept me grounded and strong, during times of turmoil.

❦

There have been a few times when I should have been smashed in a car wreck, but something (Someone) else took the wheel, and I miraculously wove in between speeding cars and came out safely on the other side of a busy, multi-lane freeway, as if the car was on autopilot. It wasn't *me* that did it, I can tell you that!

❦

I was working as a security specialist for one of the world's largest retail chains, on Christmas Eve, a few years ago. While I was standing at the front of the store, I was nervous because I needed to get some last-minute Christmas gifts, but I was out of money. There were only a couple of hours left to get everything I needed, before meeting with family the next day, out of town.

If I remember correctly, I needed $24 and some change to get what I needed, and I was desperately trying to figure out what I was going to do with little time left. I prayed for God to give me the smarts to come up with something, or work something out.

As it was nearing closing time, a man, woman and child approached me. The woman greeted me and stated that every year they go to a store and find someone who, unfortunately, has to work on Christmas Eve, and they bless that person with a gift card. She said, "This year, my son chose you."

The young boy handed me a gift card for $25.00, and I was so very thankful. My stress was gone, and I was able to get everything I needed before the store closed.

∽✧∾

The year that I decided to start tithing—something I had never done, even when I was fully engaged in church as a young man—I remember being a little worried, because the ten percent that I would be giving to the church often got me through tough times. Even so, I decided to take a leap of faith and begin tithing (and I've been tithing ever since).

Not long after, I received a much bigger raise than normal, when evaluation time came around, and I received a much better interest rate on a car loan—potentially saving me lots of money—due to the way the bank handled my loan situation!

∽✧∾

Several years ago, I was a store manager for an entertainment business. Each year, the company would hold a company-wide convention, and fly store managers from all around the world to the location. Vendors would give presentations of their new and upcoming products, we'd get a bunch of it for free (so we could better sell it), and we would have some free time to explore a new city.

I really wanted to go, but I didn't want to fly to get there, because I'm the type of guy that figures if God had wanted us to fly, he would have put wings on our backs. Plus, I'm the type who likes to be in control of his surroundings and options. But when I'm on a plane, I'm at the mercy of others who are piloting—and if something goes wrong, there's nothing I can do about it.

I'm at the airport. I check in, and everything is fine. I wait to board, and I'm still okay. I find my seat and settle in, and everything is still good. It isn't until the plane starts to taxi down the runway that I begin to get nervous. I have a window seat, on purpose, because this is my first time flying, and I want to be able to see what it's like to be up so high in the sky (bad idea).

At 30,000 feet, I felt the need for prayer. The plane was hitting turbulence, and bouncing like a school bus on an old dirt road. My eardrums felt like they were going to burst, and I was not happy about being so high off the ground—and not in control.

I prayed for a safe flight, and asked God to be with the pilots, so that they would be able to handle any situation that might arise, and then I thanked God for His blessings and truly believed that He would make everything okay.

As soon as I finished my prayer and opened my eyes, I clearly heard a little voice in my head say, "Let not your heart be troubled, nor let it be afraid."

Instantly, I was calm and relaxed. My fear had been completely removed. I smiled, thanked God, sat back in my chair and read a book throughout the rest of the flight.

My fear of flying has never returned.

❦

The Friday before Christmas, many years ago, I was driving to work on my motorcycle. It had been raining, so I grabbed my helmet. I didn't normally wear one, but I decided to do so, that day.

I was driving along, at about fifty miles-per-hour, on freshly wet pavement. As I got to the top of a small hill, I was horrified to see a car stopped in front of me, turning left.

There were cars coming toward me in the left lane, a car stopped in front of me, in my lane, and a ditch to the right. I had nowhere safe to go, so I just hit the brakes and tried to hold it steady, knowing I wasn't going to make it.

As my life was flashing before my eyes, it was as if some supernatural force violently yanked the motorcycle out from under me, and I smashed into the pavement on my left side, as everything went dark.

I was dead, at the scene.

My helmet was wrecked, on the left side. If I hadn't been wearing it, my brains would have been splattered all over the road.

My leather jacket was shredded, in the front, and down the sleeves, and my leather gloves were ripped and scarred from scraping across the pavement.

I had cracked ribs, and a dislocated rib. My abdomen was torn up, my back was cracked, and my left shoulder joint was seriously damaged.

I *know* that there is something after death, because I remember seeing myself in the middle of the road, for a very brief moment, as if I was floating at the top of one of the trees beside the road, looking down. I knew where I was and what was going on, and I must have been out for a bit, because there were cars backed up, behind me, and people had gotten out of their vehicles to check on me.

In a flash, I was back in my broken body. I began to wake up, and I could tell that the people near me were very surprised, but relieved.

As I regained consciousness, I was aware of a woman who was kneeling over me, in the middle of the road, in the rain, praying for me. She thanked God, and tried to help me.

When I came back to life, I was face-down and nothing worked. It was if someone had flipped off all the breaker switches, and turned off all the power, to every section of my body.

My hands started working, then my head and neck. It was if God had decided to send me back, and had started slowly turning me back on—rebooting me—one switch at a time, from my head down to my feet.

My arms began to work, and I got my breath back, as I managed to get my helmet off. As I began trying to push myself up, people who had been standing near me tried to help me, and I actually walked without assistance to a business that was located beside that section of highway. The woman who had been praying for me was the owner, and she helped me into a chair, gave me a cup of tea and made an emergency phone call for me.

When things calmed down, I clearly heard a heavenly voice in my head say, "It's all on you. What will you do?" That day, the direction of my life changed.

I went home and tried to relax and recover. I stood in my Man Cave, trying to breathe, but having difficulty, because the dislocated rib was poking into my left lung with every breath I took. I couldn't breathe deeply, and each breath was painful. I was terrified that I might have to have surgery.

All of a sudden, I sneezed. There was no build-up, and I didn't see it coming; it just happened, in a flash, unexpectedly.

I remember seeing stars, my knees almost buckling, and feeling like someone had stuck an ice pick into my chest. A few seconds later, the piercing pain was gone, and I could breathe freely again, because the sneeze had popped the dislocated rib back into place!

I decided to work on changing my old ways. I had a *lot* of things that needed to be fixed and improved (and still do), but I made a decision to start down that path. I prayed for strength, forgiveness and guidance.

I was given a second chance to clean up my life, and make a difference in the lives of others. I would say that's a *huge* blessing!

You have a chance, right now, also, to start a relationship with God. If you already have a relationship with Him, maybe this is your wake-up call to clean some things up in your life, or start down a path of greater involvement with the church or community—or fix things in your marriage, and get close to your spouse, again.

A happy marriage, with a loving partner, is a *tremendous* blessing—and a relationship with God can give you a solid foundation that can help you weather the storms of life.

You don't have to be perfect, and have everything in your life together, before you reach out to God. On the contrary, you will need God's wisdom, guidance and power to change your life for the better, so ask for it!

And if you think the things you've done in the past are just too awful, or you've sinned so much that God can't forgive you, you are mistaken!

Take the story of Saul, in the Bible. He made it his mission to persecute and *kill* Christians, thinking he was truly doing the work of God. He killed and imprisoned many innocent men, women and children, before the Lord spoke to Saul on the road to Damascus.

With that encounter, Saul's life completely changed; he began to preach the Gospel of Christ Jesus, wrote most of the Holy Bible's New Testament books, and began going by his Roman name of "Paul." He truly became a new creation in Christ!

If God can save a killer of Christians, transform him in such a way that he goes on to spread the Word of God throughout Rome, and write many books of the Bible, I'm sure He can handle whatever *you've* done and transform *you*, as well. Nothing is too great for God to heal and reform.

Call out to Him, profess your belief in Jesus the Savior, God's Son, that He died on a cross for your sins. Confess that you're a sinner in need of cleansing, forgiveness and healing. Invite Him into your heart and marriage. Take that first step down the path, and trust God to guide you and save you.

Find a church in your area, where you feel welcome and comfortable, and ask church leaders to help and support you.

Speaking of blessings, I have one last personal story to share with you.

I remember one of the last times I saw my maternal grandmother alive. She was in bad shape, in a nursing home, but she lit up when she saw me.

During a particular visit, we had been talking for a little while when she asked me to retrieve her purse. I handed it to her, and she reached inside and retrieved a card. "Do you remember this?" she asked, holding the card up for me to see.

It wasn't a birthday or greeting card; it was plastic, and the size of a playing card. "World's Greatest

Grandmother," or something to that effect, was printed on one side. On the other, it had a calendar for that year.

In the old days, people would carry that type of calendar card in their wallets, shirt pockets or purses, for quick reference, because there weren't any such things as personal data assistants (PDAs), tablets, personal computers or cell phones. Businesses would also give those kinds of cards away, with their logo printed on one side, as a promotional tool.

When I was a very young boy, maybe four or five years old, I wanted to get that card for my grandmother. I saw the card and knew I had to give it to her, so that she would understand just how much I loved her.

My grandmother said that she had kept the card with her, *every day*, since I gave it to her—over forty years—and that it was one of her most cherished things in all of the world. It was just a plastic card, but it meant *everything* to her.

Now, just think how much more valuable and cherished *you* are to God, being one of His children! My grandmother loved the card that was given to her by her grandson, but you are a child of the *Creator of the Universe*, and His holy book explains just how much He loves you!

It's like the story Jesus told of the Prodigal Son, in Luke 15:22-24. The son took his inheritance, left home, wasted all of his money on reckless living, and ended up nearly starving due to a famine that swept through the land.

Ultimately, the son decided that he would return to his father, beg forgiveness, admit that he made mistakes and wasn't worthy to be called "son." He would ask to be treated as a hired servant, because that's what he felt he deserved.

His father saw him coming, in the distance, and ran out to meet him. The father showed compassion, embraced and kissed his son, and prepared a feast in honor of his son's return.

Admit your own past mistakes, ask for forgiveness for the things you've done, and return to the Father. He will show you compassion and embrace you, just as the Prodigal Son's father embraced and welcomed his own son back into the family.

When you are saved from sin you are a new creation in Christ, and God no longer remembers your sin. *God doesn't dwell on your past, anymore, so why should you?*

Ask God to forgive you. Learn from your past, change your life's direction for the better, and don't let your past hold you down or define who you are *now*. You can't alter your past, but you can leave your past at the altar.

Some people may try to bring up your past, in an effort to hurt you, or get you to cast doubt on yourself and your ability to stick with your new direction. Confidently, and kindly, let them know that your past was the *old* you, not the new person you've become. Stand strong, and never let Satan cause you to doubt yourself or your new life!

And as God forgives our sins, and we make peace with ourselves, we must also forgive others, as God instructs.

Was it hard to forgive some of the people who have wronged me over the years? Yes, *very*. The hard part of forgiveness is getting yourself to the point where you actually want to do it. You feel so much better, and *lighter*, after you actually go through with it, though, because holding a grudge takes a lot of energy, and you carry a heavy load.

In attempting to forgive others, my mind would hold me back, saying that I was letting the offenders off the hook, that justice hadn't been served, or I hadn't made them feel the level of pain that *I* was feeling, yet. But all of that was just ego and emotions talking, not God and His Word.

Romans 12:19 instructs us to not avenge ourselves, because vengeance is the Lord's and *He* will deliver it. Don't worry about those who have wronged you; God will handle it all, in *His* way, in the end.

Colossians 3:13-14 says to love, and not keep a list of wrongs that have been done to you. It doesn't mean that you should continue to endure abuse, or remain in a place where your life or health may be threatened; it means that you forgive, let the nagging hurt of it fade away, and do not bring up all of the things a person has done, whenever that person irritates you or makes you angry—but do it all from a safe distance, if necessary.

If hurtful things are forgiven, and steps are being taken to improve, those things are in the past—and should be left there; the offender makes amends, and genuinely works to never repeat the same mistake, and the person who endured the offense forgives and truly lets it go.

No one is perfect, so we *all* have our rough edges. The thing that will keep us together, in all types of relationships—friends, neighbors, family, work, business, dating, marriage, etc.—is forgiveness, combined with love and understanding.

Sometimes, relationships will be forever altered, or even completely severed, but always *choose* to truly forgive.

If we are forgiving and loving, and want the family of God to grow, we will set aside our egos and pray that those who have wronged us will come to Christ, as well—and maybe *we* are the ones who need to be an example for those people, and help lead them there.

CHAPTER 51

"SO, WHERE ARE YOU NOW, DOUG?"

As I was finishing this book, I was reminded of a long drive I took to Winston-Salem, North Carolina, when I was a young man, to see a Heavy Metal concert. The headlining band was beginning to reach superstar status in the music world, and I was very excited to see their show!

I was standing on the floor, where there were no seats, in front of the stage, on the right side. The only thing separating me from the band was a young couple standing in front of me, and a metal barricade on the other side of them.

As the music started, the young guy left his petite girlfriend and went to join the mosh pit that had formed, behind us. As people were slamming into one another in the pit, they also began slamming into *us*, pushing us into the barricade—sometimes with great, sudden force. The small girl in front of me was getting hammered and crushed against the barricade, as I was being slammed and pushed into her.

She looked worried, so I instinctively put an arm out on each side of her, grabbed the barricade's bars with both hands, and created a little safe space for her, right in front of me, between my outstretched arms. I pushed back with everything I had against the bodies that were continuously slamming against my back, and that's the way we remained for nearly the entire show.

The boyfriend came back to check on her, several times, and gave a grateful nod to me, seeing that his girlfriend was being protected.

At the end of the show, they both briefly thanked me for looking out for her. I never saw them again, and never even got their names.

Protecting that girl was just something I felt compelled to do. The look on her face—that said she was truly grateful for being kept safe and comfortable—was all the thanks I needed, and I was happy that they were both able to enjoy the show, without worry.

It felt *good* to be a Good Guy—even with a few bruises. Basically, that's who I've been, my entire life, even when I was behaving like a Bad Boy. The Knight in Shining Armor has always been a big part of what makes me who I am.

There were a few times when I was younger that I was actually angry with myself, because I *wanted* to be a Bad Boy, due to hurt and betrayal, but my Good Guy side kept coming out. I'm glad that the instruction I had in my younger years made a positive impact on me, and that God's mysterious, transformative ways brought me back around to being the Good Guy that I was always meant to be.

I've made a lot of mistakes—and didn't always know how to handle certain marriage situations, in the past—but I'm much wiser, now, and I've never lost that Knight side of me. I want to be that Knight, again, for someone special. I know she's out there, and I can't wait to meet her.

Maybe this book will help to facilitate a connection, one day. Who knows? Until then, I'll just continue to live, learn and improve.

When you're praying to God for strength, understanding, patience and guidance, please say a little prayer for me, too.

AFTERWORD

Thank you for taking the time to read my personal views on Good Guys and relationships. If my writing inspires just one person to take a good, honest look at their marriage, and then work to make it better, this book will have been worth all of the time and effort that I put into it.

I used to think that if a husband and wife simply loved each other, problems would eventually work themselves out, and that love, alone, would keep them together—and I was mistaken. **Love, alone, is not enough.**

A good relationship doesn't just magically happen for most people; it takes a lot of *work*, and some compromise. Both you *and* your spouse have to be willing to do what it takes—within the boundaries of marriage, morality and respect, of course—to keep the magic and sparks alive between you.

Put your egos aside, pray for strength and guidance, open the lines of communication, regularly pray *together*, and be the best partners you can be for each other.

Learn to be there for your spouse, in the special way that he or she needs to connect with you, and work on rebuilding the wonderful relationship you once shared.

Love is a *choice*, and so is everything else you do—and every second of life is another opportunity to make a positive difference in your marriage.

With God's help, you can do anything. Never forget that.

ABOUT THE AUTHOR

Doug Kendall is an author with an impressive background. He's a non-denominational Christian, and a former business manager, political talk radio show host, political party Executive Director & congressional candidate. He knows the political system is rigged, and he has grown to have no love for government, so he has worked to find private ways of bringing positive change to his community and the people with whom he shares this planet.

For the roleplaying gamers, Doug is a multiclassing adventurer who has taken levels in Bard, Monk and Cleric, along with physical fitness, diplomacy, persuasion, writing, creative and teaching skills.

He firmly believes that "Let my people go!" is just as relevant today as it was in the days of Moses. This belief is underscored by his voluntaryist philosophy (visit voluntaryist.com for more information on voluntaryism).

Doug lives in the Pee Dee region of South Carolina. He draws inspiration from his eclectic background as a drummer, singer, songwriter and pro-freedom political activist. In his down time, he sings karaoke, designs card games, takes trips with friends, enjoys life at the beach, listens to Metal music and is a racecar driver (or so he imagines). He hopes to connect with and help people all over the world with his writing.

GOVERNMENT IS SLAVERY. TAXATION IS THEFT.

CONTACT INFORMATION

Heartflame Publishing
500 S 4th St, PO Box 2705
Hartsville, SC 29551
USA

Send email to Doug at **TheGoodGuy@minister.com**

Comments, reviews and interview requests are welcome and appreciated.

If you need help with a personal issue, please contact a licensed healthcare professional in your area.

Thank you for reading *Through the Eyes of a Good Guy.* **Please consider leaving a review on your favorite websites and social media platforms, to help expose the book to a larger audience.**

HUSBAND'S PROFILE

birthday: wedding anniversary:

birthstone: other special days:

FAVORITES

flowers: restaurants:

gemstones: meal:

snack/candy: cologne:

hobbies: music:

movie genres: vacation spots:

colors: ice cream:

book genres: games:

stores: jewelry:

sports teams: other:

Husband, complete this sentence:
I feel most loved when my wife

My idea of a perfect date night:

WIFE'S PROFILE

birthday: wedding anniversary:

birthstone: other special days:

FAVORITES

flowers: restaurants:

gemstones: meal:

snack/candy: perfume:

hobbies: music:

movie genres: vacation spots:

colors: ice cream:

book genres: games:

stores: jewelry:

sports teams: other:

Wife, complete this sentence:
I feel most loved when my husband

My idea of a perfect date night: